The Heart of an Orphan

Amy Eldridge

First edition

Cover Photograph by Zhang Ming

Back Photograph by Kelci Cox

ISBN 978-0-9794639-3-8

To my wonderful children –

To the moon and back, always

One

Defining Moments

I think when we look back over our lives, we will all see those "defining moments" which changed the course of our existence forever. Of course, most people would mention the day they were married or the moment they first laid eyes on their child, but I believe all of us have other events which make such an enormous impact on our hearts that the path we thought was clearly in front of us is altered in significant ways. The curious thing about those moments is that we don't usually see them coming. We don't wake up that morning thinking our lives will suddenly be transformed, and yet a moment in time can do just that. The decisions we make in those periods of time can then shape the very essence of who we are. I know for certain that one of my own defining moments came the day I walked into a Chinese orphanage for the first time, when life as I knew it changed forever.

At the time, I was the mother of six children – five the old-fashioned way and one adopted from China. If you need an example of a stay-at-home mom, I think I probably fit the bill: Girl Scout leader, classroom helper, high school youth group volunteer. My days were spent running kids to activities all over central Oklahoma in my 12-passenger red van. I was super busy with being a mother, and in my mind quite content.

My youngest child at the time was Anna, a precocious three-year-old who talked nonstop. She had been adopted as a baby from an orphanage in southern China, and, as soon as she began speaking, she started asking questions about her early life there. Questions I simply couldn't answer as I wasn't allowed to visit her orphanage on my overseas adoption trip. All I knew about life in institutional care came from books and reading other people's blogs. Anna's questions were deep – far deeper than the typical kids' questions I normally answered about bugs or rainbows or why it isn't a good idea to put beans up your nose. She was my sixth child; so I thought I had the standard preschool questions down pat, but Anna asked questions well beyond her years. She wanted to know who took care of her in China and what her daily life was like, and her curiosity grew deeper every day. Time and again, I had to answer her increasingly pointed questions with the same three words: *"I don't know."*

Before she joined our family, I had read many books about the best ways to speak to your child if he or she was adopted, and so, from the first days that I held her in my arms, I would quietly tell her how she came to be with me. We would sit together on our white porch swing, and I would repeat her story again and again so there would never be a moment she didn't know about her beginnings. She would lay her head on my shoulder while I began the soon familiar tale: "You were born in China, an ancient country of beauty and dragons. You were born to a woman there we will always honor because she gave you life...." Anna went from babydom to toddlerhood to preschool hearing about her adoption, but the reality is that the sum total of her China story was no more than a simple paragraph.

I will never forget sitting by the side of the tub one evening when she was taking a bath. She looked at me with her beautiful brown eyes and asked, "Do you think they loved me?" I knew immediately who "they" were: her birth parents, who had placed her in a straw basket in the early morning hours of her birth and walked away, leaving a one-day-old baby all alone on the sidewalk. There was no note, no explanation, and, even at age three, my daughter was realizing that there were holes in her life story which she needed to fill.

I looked at her trusting face that night and knew as her mom, it was my obligation to try and help her get any answers we could, even while realizing there was only one place where those keys might be found. Just a few months later, I found myself boarding a plane to her birth city in China, praying that somehow I could learn more about my daughter's beginnings but understanding that I had absolutely no idea of what I would discover there.

It is always intriguing to me how different people can experience the same sort of life event and come out of it differently. Some people experience divorce, for example, and come back resilient and hoping for second love, while others go through the experience and close themselves off to new relationships forever. Or two children can attend their very first musical performance, and one can come home saying he squirmed with boredom the whole show while the other sits in the darkened theater breathless with the realization that being on stage is where she is meant to be. Obviously thousands of people visit orphanages every year and are able to return to their lives back home quite fine, but, for me, walking into my daughter's orphanage for the very first time changed everything I thought I knew about my life.

I woke up at 3 a.m. that fateful morning in her birth city because of jet lag, but also because I felt electrified that the day had finally come when I would see Anna's first home. I lay in the bed with a million thoughts running through my mind about

3

what I was soon to see. I began praying that God would open the doors that were meant to be open and give closure to the questions for Anna that could never be answered. I was actually crying as I left for the orphanage, feeling truly overwhelmed that I was being given the opportunity to meet those who had cared for my daughter. It had taken many months to get permission to visit, but it only took a few minutes by taxi to pull up into the orphanage courtyard, which was flanked by multi-colored flags and the words "Children's Paradise" over the front door. The building itself was six stories high, and, as I looked up, I could see about 20 children in the windows above me watching my arrival guardedly through metal bars. I took a deep breath as I stepped inside the entrance.

The first thing I can remember registering was that the entire building was so very quiet. I knew over a hundred children lived in the orphanage, and so the strange silence struck my heart almost immediately. I was met at the bottom of the stairs by one of the women who had brought Anna to me at my hotel many years earlier on my adoption trip. She warmly welcomed me as a guest of the orphanage and then led me upstairs past row after row of metal baby cribs, filled with abandoned children staring solemnly at me with their dark eyes. They didn't make a sound. I know it probably sounds cliché to say that it was like time moving in slow motion, but my mind was struggling to fully grasp that all the children surrounding me had no parents to care for them.

One of the orphanage staff members took my arm and led me to Anna's baby room, pointing to a crib that she had supposedly slept in. I was overcome with emotion picturing my now loud and vivacious daughter in this eerily quiet room. In that moment, it became so absolute to me that my child had been **orphaned**. I know that sounds ridiculous since, of course, I had adopted her because of that reality. But it was honestly

4

just an abstract concept to me before. Now I was standing in my daughter's exact room in front of a blue metal crib, staring down at a new little baby lying exactly where she had as well. It is so easy as adoptive parents to think our kids' lives start when they meet us, but it finally hit me in that moment that my daughter had lived through something no baby should experience. During the first few days of her life, she had lost her parents. She was left all alone in the night on a village street. She was picked up by the police and then placed into an institution.

I tried to soak in everything I could for her that day so that I could fully tell her about where she had come from. Her room was cold but clean, with very Spartan conditions and white walls. The babies were all bundled in threadbare snowsuits and blankets, lying flat on their backs in the crib on straw mats. I had never thought about whether she had been cold as a baby as heat is something most Westerners take for granted. I was told that most orphanages in China at that time didn't have heating systems. Even though I was in southern China, the orphanage on that January day was extremely cold. The nannies began picking up babies for me to see, and their little cheeks were all red and chapped from the winter air. I held baby after baby, and so many of them would lock their eyes into mine, wanting to make that human connection. One of the hardest moments was when I picked up a little girl in a yellow snowsuit named LuLu. Her black hair was sticking straight up in all directions, and she snuggled into my neck with all of her might. Just a few moments after I had her in my arms, I was told we had to move onto another room. I reluctantly went to put her down, but she just clung onto me, her eyes welling up with tears when I tried to lay her back down in the crib. As a mom, there was something so inherently wrong with putting down a baby who so obviously needed to be held, as when I released my hands from her body she began to sob loudly. Everything in my heart was telling me to go back and scoop her back up again, but I was told firmly it was time for us to leave. As I headed down the steps to the floor below, I could still hear her piercing cries echoing in the hallway.

On the next floor, I was taken to one of the toddler rooms, where the children were sitting at little tables getting ready to have their first of two meals that day. I watched as the nanny placed a tiny metal bowl filled with white rice in front of each child. The children looked at me warily but then began to eat. One little girl who was extremely thin caught my eye. I knelt down to her level, quickly noticing that her lips and hands were a deep blue. I gently took her little hand in mine, and her tiny fingers were like ice. Her eyes were impossible to describe. So incredibly beautiful, but so very solemn. I looked down at the little girl's bowl and saw she had eaten all of her rice, and then she began scraping the sides of the bowl trying to get every last grain. All of the children were looking at me now, and I asked if it would be okay to give the kids an extra treat I had brought, some pork jerky bought from a street vendor on the way to the orphanage. When the bag was pulled out, every eye in the room locked onto it.

I took out a piece of the jerky and ripped off a small amount to give to the little blue girl. When the other children saw the meat in my hand, their little mouths dropped open like baby birds, holding their breaths hoping I would put something inside. I walked child to child, hand feeding every one, and I will never forget the emotions that washed over me as I realized just how hungry they were. I got down on my knees to hand out the food, and a little girl with a strawberry birthmark over half of her face came up to me. She looked to be about three. Her eyes definitely told me she didn't trust me, but she bravely put out one hand to take a piece of meat. She then quietly sized me up and slowly put out her other hand. I put a piece there too. I could see the wheels spinning in her head on how she could possibly get even more, and then she slowly opened up her mouth to let me put a third piece on her tongue. I don't ever want to forget that moment, as, in that quiet room of toddlers waiting anxiously for me to feed them, God began turning my heart inside out.

Later that morning, I was taken to one of the baby rooms on the main floor of the orphanage. The staff doctor, an incredibly kind man named Dr. Huang, took me to the back right corner to see a baby boy whose skin was clearly blue, just like the little girl I had met earlier. Dr. Huang pointed his hand to the baby's chest and shook his head sadly. Everything now clicked together for me, and I realized that both of these children were suffering from heart disease. Gazing down at the little boy, I found it hard to process that I was standing right there looking at a child who was dying. I naively asked when his heart surgery would be, only to be told that there weren't funds available to save his life. The orphanage had recently used up all their money to send a different little boy for surgery, and so there wasn't anything left to help the baby in front of me. I asked his name and age and was told that baby Kang was only nine months old. The doctor explained that Kang's skin was so dark because he was struggling to get the oxygen he needed. Dr. Huang shook his head sadly again, and, as I stood holding this precious baby, I felt something in my own heart break in two. As a Westerner, the harsh reality of the situation was hard for me to take in. From what I knew about healthcare in America, if a child was dying and needed medical treatment, it was given no matter what. Only afterwards would come the big question of how it would be paid for. What I was learning about medical care in China at that time was that without payment up front, there simply was no surgery. It was hard to believe that the baby

I was now holding would just pass away unless the orphanage could somehow come up with the funding needed. I put my hand on the little boy's head and said a silent prayer that somehow his life would be saved.

I returned back to the U.S. and tried everything in my power to go back to life as usual, but I couldn't get the children I had met in the orphanage out of my mind. Their faces never left my thoughts. I wrote in my journal:

I am having such a hard time now that I am home as my mind fully starts to comprehend all that I saw. How could I have not known the conditions that children around the world are facing? How could I take so much for granted and not realize the blessings my kids and I have been given?

It was impossible for me to sleep, and, as I tried to go about my daily life, it seemed like I was walking through quicksand. I took Anna to the playground one afternoon. As I looked around at all the smiling and playing kids, I felt a blanket of heaviness come over my heart. All around me were parents who seemed oblivious to just how extraordinary this everyday moment was; in fact, most looked quite bored. I wanted to run up to them and say, "Do you not see how amazing it is that you are here with your kids, and that they are healthy and warmly dressed? Do you not see how incredibly fortunate it is that your child's only worry at the moment isn't true hunger or trying to breathe, but simply getting to the top of the slide?" But they were exactly who I was, just a week before, completely unaware of how many children around the world are living in hard conditions – cold and malnourished, and even struggling to take their next breath. Once again that night, I found myself unable to sleep, remembering the tiny baby's face I had seen in the orphanage that was dangerously blue. At 2 a.m., I pushed back the covers on my bed and went to the computer, feeling woefully inadequate at what I was about to try. I took a deep breath and typed two little words into the search engine: BABY HEARTS. In that moment the course of my life changed forever as my journey to bring healing to those who are orphaned began.

Two

A Leap of Faith

By now probably everyone has heard the saying that it "takes a village" to raise a child. I quickly learned as I tried to get help for baby Kang that it would take a village to save a child's life as well. One of the first things I did the next day was to write an email to my friends and family, letting them know about Kang and that he would most likely pass away without heart surgery. I had never done anything like this before. I'm one of those people who rarely ask for help because I don't like being a burden to anyone. But I thought about all the times someone had come to my door asking me to contribute to some fundraising effort or another, and I always gave a little. I realized that it was finally my turn to be the one asking, and so I typed:

I never could have prepared myself for the impact my recent trip to China would have on my heart. I keep returning again and again to prayer and my faith because, while it seems so overwhelming to me, I know that nothing is overwhelming to God. I know that I need to just take baby step after baby step to try and set things in motion to help the kids I met in China. I am humbled every single time I walk in the door to my house, knowing that I have a home with heat and hot water and family to hug me, while the orphaned kids I met have none of the above. I was colder than I have ever been before in China, and those kids in the orphanage wake up and go to bed every single night with no heat and little food.

I keep being reminded of the story about the little boy who is standing on the sand throwing starfish that had washed up on shore back into the sea. An old man walked by and saw this little boy throwing them back one by one, and he commented to the child that there were thousands washed up, and what difference could he possibly be making. The little boy picked up another starfish, threw it back into the water and said, "I made a difference to that one." I keep hearing this over and over in my head, and I know that I can't help every orphan in China. But I know for certain that I need to try and help one particular child.

On my trip, I met a tiny baby boy who is slowly dying in the orphanage because his heart is bad. The main doctor at the orphanage is such a kind and compassionate man, and he pulled me over to this little boy and told me with great sadness that they don't have the money needed to arrange for this child to have surgery. It is a humbling and sobering experience to hold a little child in your hands that is so ill with no hope of getting medical treatment. I am crying again as I write this because I can remember every detail about his perfect little face. His mother and father abandoned him simply because he had the bad luck to be born with a heart defect. I held him and thought I could not let this same defect also take his life.

I have never in my life done anything like this before, but I realized that I cannot do this alone, and so I am asking all of my friends to please consider sending a donation, no matter how small, so that I can get the funds to the orphanage for this little boy to have surgery. I know that $5 can become $10 and *then $50 and then $100 when people open their hearts and join together for a worthwhile goal. Please know that I will accept even one dollar with so much joy... because it puts me that much closer to being able to save this child's life.*

To say that the Internet has transformed our lives is a true understatement, isn't it? With one quick keystroke, my letter was sent to everyone in my address book, and I took a very deep breath and prayed that God would let my words reach the right people. Incredibly, my letter began being passed from one online group to the next, and I began getting messages from complete strangers asking how they could help. An adoptive mom in Colorado, whose child was from the same orphanage as my daughter and Baby Kang, contacted me to let me know that Dr. Max Mitchell, a pediatric heart surgeon from Denver, was actually going to China the very next month to perform heart surgery on orphans there. Could Kang possibly be added to his surgery schedule? She gave me all of his contact information, and within days I was able to connect with him. It was very clear in speaking with him that Dr. Mitchell was a remarkable physician with a true heart for service. He told me that he would be happy to consider adding Baby Kang to his surgery schedule, but he said he would first need to see the medical files in order to see what type of heart defect he had and what type of operation he would need.

When I requested Kang's medical records from the orphanage, I quickly received back the files of THREE children in their care who needed their hearts repaired. You have to admire the staff there for doing everything possible to get help for all the kids. One of the files was for the tiny little girl I had met during mealtime at the orphanage, the "little blue girl." I stared in disbelief at the file which listed Zhen's age as five years old. She was the size of toddler – and a very thin toddler at that. I couldn't believe she could possibly be five and struggled to take in how urgently she needed surgery as well. The other file was for a two-year-old boy named Qiang, who had a large hole between the chambers of his heart ventricles. The orphanage told me that he frequently turned gray and had spells where he couldn't breathe. The weight I was feeling on my shoulders to help baby Kang intensified immediately times three, as did the amount of money we would need in order to make the surgeries possible. Dr. Mitchell was donating his time and skills to heal the children's hearts, but we would still have to pay the hospital for the operating room time, nursing staff, and medications. Each child's surgery was estimated to cost between $5,000 and $7,000, which at the time seemed entirely beyond our reach. You might as well have asked me to help raise a million dollars as I had never even been comfortable asking my neighbors to give $10 for a school fundraiser. I was the mom who would sit down instead and write a check for my kids' contribution versus having to ask anyone for money. Now we needed $15,000 to $20,000 in order to save the lives of three children in a Chinese orphanage. It truly seemed impossible, but, of course, now I know that it is in those inconceivable moments that we get to see the extraordinary occur.

How many times in your life have you been pushed completely out of your comfort zone? When I look back on myself during that time, I can see so clearly now that I was living on "cruise control." My life with my kids was predictable and safe, and we had a routine that revolved squarely around ourselves. I was basically on autopilot, and so it was quite terrifying to think of stepping out in faith to try and arrange heart surgeries for not one, but three children. Why in the world would I think this was possible? How could a mom in Oklahoma 8,000 miles away really make that happen? And yet thankfully (oh so thankfully!), I came to understand that it wasn't all up to me, and it certainly wasn't ABOUT me. This was only about the children.

You may or may not be surprised to learn that there are many people in America who believe that we should only help those within our own borders. In fact, now I know that of all the money that people and corporations give to charity each year less than 10% goes to help internationally. Even some of the people I thought I knew well began telling me that they could only support my efforts if the money stayed locally as if saving a child's life outside of the U.S. somehow wasn't as worthy as saving a child in an orphanage overseas. I will be honest and say that I began to have many doubts, especially when I counted up the pledges for Kang so far and realized we were nowhere close to funding even the first surgery. One day when I was praying, I felt three simple words spoken to my heart: "**Every child counts**." Not just those in the U.S. or those fortunate enough to be born healthy, or those with a bright future already in front of them, but every single child who enters this world, regardless of location, circumstance, or special need. I sat quietly for a few moments to let the weight of those words settle deeply inside me. I didn't know it then, but those three words would someday go on to impact many lives. At the moment, I took a deep breath and reminded myself that Kang, Zhen, and Qiang had been given up by their parents most likely because their heart defects were more than they could handle. We couldn't give up as well. All three kids needed to have surgery because undeniably their lives truly mattered. Thankfully, I was soon to discover that this world is filled with amazing and generous people all around us, if we will only find the courage to speak up for those in need.

I tripled my efforts to call and email everyone I knew, asking if they could help the kids get surgery, while my initial plea for Kang continued to wing its way around the globe.

Countless online friends came alongside me, committed to making these surgeries happen, and soon there was a massive grassroots effort underway. A few days later, I went to my mailbox and was amazed to see almost a dozen envelopes from people I didn't even know. Each one had a small note of caring for Baby Kang, along with a donation to help him get surgery. The next day there were 20 letters, then 50, and finally the mailman came to my door with over 100 envelopes, all for Baby Kang. I would sit at my kitchen table each day opening up the letters and notes with tears running down my face. I felt like I was in the final scene of "It's a Wonderful Life" with perfect strangers coming up to say, "Of course we can help."

Within days, Baby Kang's surgery was completely funded, but the clock was ticking quickly on whether we could raise enough in time for the other two children to be healed. Zhen, the beautiful little girl who was so blue, had such a severe heart condition that Dr. Mitchell told me she would need extra surgical exams done first, since there was a chance her heart was too complex to be repaired. Then there were the increasing logistics of how you even move three orphaned children across provincial lines. The kids were in southern China, and they would need to travel north in order to receive help from Dr. Mitchell. None of the kids had official IDs which would allow them to board a plane, but going by air seemed to be the only option as the journey by train would be too long and hard for children that ill. Should we go ahead and book flights without the funds being fully raised? The air tickets were nonrefundable but were selling out fast.

With just ten days to go before the surgeries, I received an email which just about made me fall out of my chair.

Hi Amy,

My husband and I want to pay for one of the children's surgeries. I mailed the check this morning to you for $5,000.00. My husband got a bonus at the end of the year, and I have been praying where God wants us to use it. I also have passed the word out to others to pray about helping, so let's see what God does next.

P.S. You might want to get a flight for all the kids. :)

The very next day I got a phone call from a woman in Chicago, who had actually received my email from a friend in Canada. She said that she had an overwhelming feeling that she needed to call me and offer help as she had open heart surgery twice as a child. She said she almost couldn't breathe because the weight of these kids getting the surgeries they needed was so fully on her. She had tried to help a little girl with a heart problem the previous year in China, but that little girl had tragically died before medical help could reach her. She told me she was going to sell her car to come up with the rest of the money we needed since "a car has no eternal worth at all, but a child's life is priceless."

I explained that miraculously we had raised everything we needed except the final $800, and she told me she was going to walk to her mailbox right that very moment to send a check for that amount. She ended the call by telling me to never forget that true riches only come from helping others.

I hung up the phone in stunned silence and complete awe. It was done. In three short weeks, all the funds needed to give Kang, Zhen, and Qiang a chance at being healed had been raised. The most beautiful part of it to me was that an entire community of compassionate people, from all over the world, had come together to make it happen. Family, friends, and perfect strangers cared enough about three children they had never seen in person to make the impossible possible.

Three

The First Surgeries

Plans were made for the children and their caregivers to fly to Hangzhou the first week of March, after resolving numerous logistical issues of securing oxygen for the flight and making sure the airline would even allow children that ill to fly. Little Zhen needed to arrive a few days earlier than the other kids because she first needed a heart catheterization, a procedure where doctors would put a thin, hollow tube through a cut in her thigh and then thread the tube to her heart to get a better understanding of its issues. Since Zhen was already five and possibly had the most complex heart condition of the three, Dr. Mitchell felt this test was essential before attempting surgery.

The nannies knew that the weather up north would be much colder than at home; so they bundled up Zhen in so many layers that she could hardly walk. The aunties who were traveling with the kids to Hangzhou were both excited and nervous at the same time; none of them had ever been on an airplane before. Emotions were running very high for everyone as the reality hit that the precious children in their care were soon to undergo open heart surgery. Zhen gave the cold shoulder to her nanny because she was so upset that she had been taken away from her friends to a strange place. She actually refused to speak at all, no matter how hard the nanny tried to reassure her. A few days later when her friend Qiang finally arrived in Hangzhou as well, Zhen finally broke her silence. She was so happy to see her orphanage mate again and quickly asked, "Where are our friends? Why have they brought us here?"

Dr. Mitchell explained to me that Zhen's heart cath showed she had a very rare but very serious heart defect called Transposition of the Great Arteries (TGA). This means that the two main arteries leaving her heart were reversed, changing her blood circulation and leaving her severely short of oxygen, resulting in her deep blue coloring. Ideally, this condition is often treated within days after birth as, without a good supply of oxygen-rich blood, a child's body can suffer severe complications and, of course, even death. That is why Zhen was unable to walk across her small room in the orphanage without having to kneel down to try and catch her breath. If you look up this condition on the Internet, you will see that every medical article says, "All INFANTS require surgery for survival." Yet somehow little Zhen had managed to live five years with this severe heart condition. Dr. Mitchell explained that her surgery would be quite complex, and so he had decided to put her first on the schedule.

All of us who were involved with the preparations could not believe that the time had finally come for the kids to receive their operations. I couldn't sleep at all and found myself pacing back and forth as the hours slowly ticked closer to when the first child would have surgery. The night before Zhen's operation, I received a call from my friend Tingting, who was at the hospital with the kids. "It's snowing," she said with excitement, "and snow is a sign of good luck in China!" She told me that all of the children had gone to the window to see the flakes gently falling down. Since they were from the south part of China, it was the very first time they had ever seen snow.

As I prayed that night for their healing, I kept that poignant image of them in my mind of their noses pressed up against the hospital room window, looking out in wonder at the snow. A sign of good luck... and it was indeed as the next afternoon I got the blessed phone call I had been waiting for. Zhen's surgery had gone perfectly, and Dr. Mitchell told me the "little blue girl" was now a beautiful shade of pink.

The next child on the operating schedule was two-year-old Qiang, who had actually been enjoying his time in the hospital as the nannies kept giving him lots of attention and good food to stay strong. The following day I once again got an excited phone call that his surgery had gone exactly as planned. No surprises at all, and the doctors felt his heart was fully repaired. I have to admit that right about that time I began thinking that heart surgery always goes perfectly. You have to remember that I had never even seen a child with heart disease before Kang, and so I was extremely naïve at that time about all the post-operative complications that can occur when a surgeon opens up the very organ which gives us life. I went to bed the night before Kang's surgery basically floating on air, confident that in just one more day all three children would be healed. All three kids could then return to their orphanage with new and healthy lives in front of them.

Dr. Mitchell had operated on many orphaned children that week in Hangzhou, and he had scheduled Kang's case for the final day since the baby was younger and had a more commonly seen heart defect – Tetralogy of Fallot. TOF is a congenital condition involving four defects of the heart. Babies with this special need often have blue skin, difficulty breathing, and poor weight gain – all symptoms we saw in little Kang. Dr. Mitchell felt the baby was a great candidate for a full repair, however, and assured me things should go well. Since Kang was the baby who "started it all," I found myself pacing the whole next day while waiting for news. When I went to pick up my kids from school, I must have crossed the wide playground at least a dozen times as I simply couldn't keep still. Why hadn't they called yet? Did they forget to let me know how things went in their excitement of having all the surgeries done? It was now almost 4 a.m. the next day in China, and normally they called me with updates by nighttime. Finally my phone rang, and I answered breathlessly asking how Kang had done. It took me a few moments to fully grasp what I was hearing, and I sank to my knees on the concrete with the news. We needed to pray urgently for Baby Kang. He was in critical condition post-op and sinking fast.

Four

Baby Kang

The next few days were an absolute blur to me. Kang's small body was filling with fluid, and he had slipped into a coma. I was able to speak briefly with Dr. Mitchell on his last day at the hospital, and he shared his frustrations with me about the case as the information he had been given of Kang's heart anatomy before surgery ended up being incorrect. When he had cut into Kang's heart, the holes weren't where the echo had indicated. I listened without taking a single breath while he explained that his only option at that moment was to hold Kang's tiny heart in his hand in order to FEEL the vibrations so he could know where the repair was needed. What a powerful image that was, of a grown man cradling a baby's heart and "listening" with his hands for the best way to bring healing. Dr. Mitchell tried to reassure me, telling me the repair was a good one, but he explained that the sudden change in Kang's blood flow had caused him serious post-op complications. His last words to me before hanging up were that I needed to prepare myself for the very real possibility that Kang could pass away.

Up to this point, those of us who had helped make the arrangements for surgery had been merely observers as all the decisions for the children's actual medical care had, of course, been made by Dr. Mitchell. Now that he was leaving the hospital, I was about to learn very quickly just how differently decisions are made for patients in China, where a "pay as you go" medical system is the norm. We had only sent enough funds to the hospital for Kang's surgery to be done but not enough for any extended post-op care. Every additional day he stayed in the ICU raised his costs significantly, and, since he was in a coma, the hospital now wanted a guarantee that his bill would be covered if they kept him on life support.

We were extremely fortunate that the Chinese physician who took over Kang's care when Dr. Mitchell left spoke English. He and I were able to speak by phone about Kang's worsening situation, and he explained that Kang's kidneys had begun to shut down. He wanted to know what my decision was on the next steps for the baby. I'm sure I must have sounded very confused on the phone. What did he mean by "MY decision?" Kang's medical care wasn't my decision. I was in Oklahoma getting updates by phone. Wasn't it the doctor's decision? Or the orphanage staff's decision? I didn't know anything about comas and organ failure, but the doctor explained that since I was the one technically paying Kang's bills, the decision for continued care was firmly mine to make. The orphanage director had agreed. Since it was "our" money being spent, they all felt it was our decision on what to do next. When I asked what the options were, I was told that it was a long shot and not routinely done at the hospital but perhaps kidney dialysis could help Kang's body turn the corner. Did I want them to rent a dialysis machine? Did we have enough funds to cover any additional efforts to save his life?

I immediately said, "Do the dialysis!" – because that's what anyone would say, right? We tell doctors to do whatever it takes to make a child get better. Americans often have the mindset of "act now, pay later," which is very different from the much more pragmatic approach of many in China. The dialysis machine was wheeled into Kang's hospital room to keep him alive for another day, clearing toxins from his body, while he remained unresponsive. The next morning I received another phone call – this time to explain that perhaps the baby's kidneys had already suffered too much damage. He was an orphan after all, and perhaps I was simply extending the inevitable. No orphanage would be able to provide long-term dialysis for a child in their care; so did I really want to pay for yet another session? Without normal kidney function, of course, he would pass away in an orphanage. Perhaps any additional funds we had left would be better spent helping another child, who wasn't in critical condition. Maybe I should take a few hours to think about it and then call back with my decision.

I hung up with my heart pounding over the sobering news. How could this be happening? Kang was the baby we had originally set out to save, and yet right at that moment he was battling for his very life. Once again I turned to my computer and the community of people around the world who had been so supportive of getting Kang the surgery he needed. I wrote:

Could everyone please just lift this little child up? He doesn't have a mother or a father, but I know he has people all over the world rallying behind him and wishing him well. He has no idea how many people are praying, so if he would pass away within the next day... let it be with complete love surrounding him. I keep trying to find any sort of peace in knowing that if Kang's life does end, he will be treasured in heaven and finally warm and not hungry. But I selfishly want him to experience that first right here on earth, with parents who would love him and who would tell him how wonderful he is. I want to hold him again myself. I don't want to know what

25

happens to an orphan who dies in China. I want his life to count.
He IS important. His life DOES matter.

A few hours after sending my request for prayers, I received another urgent call from China. The heart surgeon told me that Kang had taken a turn for the worse, and his only hope of surviving was another radical surgery. Did we want to move forward even though he could possibly die immediately on the table once his chest was reopened? I was so completely out of my depth in knowing what was best right now, and I told the doctor honestly that I didn't know what to do. I wanted to speak to Dr. Mitchell first, and so I hung up quickly to try and reach him somehow, but his flight had already left Beijing. It was actually scheduled to land in San Francisco at any moment, however, and so I sent a frantic email to everyone I knew: "PLEASE start calling any number you can think of with United Airlines. We need to have Dr. Mitchell paged when he lands in San Francisco in 20 minutes. United flight 858... scheduled to land at 7:08. He has to call me ASAP. Tell them to have him call Amy Eldridge, and that it's truly a matter of life and death."

I am sure that is a day that those working the switchboard with United remembered for a while as countless people began calling with the same message: Paging Dr. Mitchell. Life or death emergency. Later he would tell me that when he got off the plane at the gate, he heard his name on the overhead speaker literally every few seconds as so many people had called to put in the same message that it was now on a continual loop. It definitely wasn't the welcome he was expecting after a 12 hour flight from overseas, but he called me the moment he cleared immigration, and I explained what I had been told about Kang's current situation. Dr. Mitchell agreed with the surgeon in China; Kang's only chance was to be taken back to the OR

26

immediately. A wide opening would be cut in one of his major heart vessels. It was his final hope.

Baby Kang, still in a coma, somehow managed to find the strength to come through that second surgery, and this time the doctors decided to keep his chest wall completely open rather than stitching it closed post surgery. The good news was that his heart function looked beautiful after the second operation. His blood pressure had stabilized, and his heart was beating at a very strong 170 beats per minute. The surgeon told me that if Kang could survive just 48 more hours with the help of dialysis, then he believed the little boy would finally be on the road to recovery. Thankfully each update after that one became a little more positive. Dr. Mitchell kept in daily contact with the surgeons in China, and finally came the wonderful news we had been praying for: Kang's kidneys had begun working on their own again. He was officially out of the woods, and his chest cavity could finally be closed.

Six weeks after he had made the biggest journey of his life so far, Kang was declared healed. He now had a wide incision stretching from his neck to his abdomen, but his blue lips and fingers were a thing of the past. The tiny baby who had inspired me to step firmly out of my comfort zone was finally heading back to his orphanage with a strong and healthy heart.

Five

Zhen

A few weeks after the heart surgeries took place, I made a return trip to China to see the other children who had been healed. Little Kang was still in the hospital at that time, but I was really looking forward to seeing Zhen and Qiang back at the orphanage. On my first trip to my daughter's birth city, I think I was so overwhelmed by everything I was trying to take in that I never even asked about the individual life stories of the children I was meeting. Many of us are probably guilty of this when we hear reports on the news about world happenings or social events. We hear about the children in war-torn temporary camps, for example, and many times our minds lump them all together as a collective group: refugees. Or we read about children growing up in the projects of inner city Chicago, yet they remain nameless and faceless in our minds. We say, "That's awful; they deserve better," but it's almost impossible for us to come away from those news articles fully understanding what it is like to be an individual child in those circumstances. I have since realized that one of the problems with seeing children as a collective group is that we are less likely to take action to help them when we don't see them for the unique, important human beings they are. Every child on this earth has huge hopes and dreams just waiting to be realized, but it is easier to ignore them when they don't have a name and when you don't know their individual stories. Up until this point, I know I was still thinking of the kids I met as some sort of group unit, *"the orphans."* I am so thankful that during this second trip to my daughter's first home, I began to fully understand just how much I had missed by not doing my best to get to know each individual child.

As soon as I entered the orphanage, I spotted Zhen, formerly known as the little blue girl. She was sitting on her caregiver's lap, and she solemnly stared at me as I came up to get closer. Her skin still had a slightly purple hue to it, but it was so much lighter than before. I asked if I could see where her operation had been, and she studied me with a great deal of seriousness before nodding that it was okay. She pulled up her shirt to show me a giant red scar that ran the entire length of her very skinny chest. She was so thin and tiny that she looked like she might break at any moment, but the nannies told me she was feeling so much better now and that she no longer got winded when walking. Before the operation, she would cry frequently, pointing to her chest and saying "it hurts" when she couldn't catch her breath. But now she never complained of any pain.

All I had known before the surgery was that she was a five-year-old girl who was far too tiny and blue. That was my full knowledge of this living, breathing child who now sat quietly beside me. When I asked the nannies if they would please tell me her story, I sadly learned just how much she had already been through in her short life. Zhen had been abandoned just six months before. When she had been brought to the orphanage, she was absolutely terrified and wouldn't speak. It was terrible to think that she had been left with the full knowledge in her heart and mind of who her parents were and what she had suddenly lost. When I was going through the adoption process for my daughter, all I had read regarding China and the one child policy was about infant abandonment, and I think that is the image many people had in their minds – of families abandoning a baby daughter due to being born female. I honestly had never thought about older child abandonment before, but I would quickly learn that thousands of older children are left each year in China, often due to being born with medical needs. I listened to Zhen's story, knowing I had a little boy of my own near her age at the time, who was at that very moment waiting for me to return home. I sat there thinking about how much it would hurt him if I disappeared in an instant, with no explanation at all, and how bewildered he would be if the police suddenly came to take him to a large building filled with perfect strangers and said, "This is where you'll live now." Can you even imagine how frightening that would be to a little child? And yet here was Zhen, sitting quietly in front of me, staring at me with her solemn eyes, and she had lived through that exact nightmare of suddenly finding herself all alone and being taken by police to a social welfare institution. In addition to losing her parents, of course, she was also extremely ill, getting short of breath and feeling winded if she even tried to walk across the room. I had no idea she had so recently arrived to the orphanage when I had worked to arrange her medical care. Just a few months after losing her parents, Zhen had been taken to a strange new hospital for open heart surgery. How was she processing it all? What had been going through her mind?

Slowly that day, she began to come out of her shell with me. I saw Zhen's first giggles, and I learned that she really liked pretty clothes. I had brought her a Disney princess shirt, which thankfully made me rise up in status in her book. Finally she came over to sit on my lap, confirming that she was no heavier than a baby bird. We sat there together, and I tried to imagine what it took to permanently walk away from this absolutely precious little girl. Perhaps her parents had panicked when she became so very sick, or perhaps they had no money to help her become well. She looked up at me and blessed me with a tiny little grin, and I wished more than anything that there was some way for her mom to know she had received surgery. I wished there was some magic way to let her know that the daughter she had known and cared for these last five years was safe and sitting on my lap. But, of course, there was no way to make that a reality as the ads the orphanage had placed in the newspaper stating she had been found had gone unanswered.

In China, when a child has been left and then discovered by the police, an orphanage is supposed to place a "finding ad," which has a photo of the child and short details of where the child was found. In order for a child to be legally registered for adoption, the finding ad must run for three months. Then if no birthparents come forward, the government can designate the child a ward of the state. Only then is the child potentially eligible to be adopted by a new family. When Zhen's parents did not come forward, the orphanage staff decided she would be registered for international adoption. I was so hopeful that a new family would step forward for her.

A few months later when her adoption file was released, I spoke again with Dr. Mitchell because I wanted to be able to talk to any potential parents about Zhen's prognosis. He explained carefully to me that the heart defect she had been born with was an extremely serious one and that she would need additional surgeries in the future. He told me frankly that, with her condition, she might even need a heart transplant to live into adulthood. I was crushed to hear the news. Would any family be willing to take on that very real risk?

Soon after her adoption file became available, I received a phone call from a woman who had followed the original surgeries. She told me that her family was considering adopting

Zhen, and she wanted to get more information from me so it could possibly help with their decision. It had only been a few days since I had spoken to Dr. Mitchell, who had given me the very realistic but grim view of what Zhen's future might be. I took a deep breath and told the woman on the phone what he had explained to me – that Zhen might not live until adulthood without intense intervention, and even then no one could promise she would survive. I told her I understood that most families would probably find it very hard to knowingly walk into that situation through adoption. There was a brief pause on the phone, and I prepared myself for the woman to tell me it would be too much to take on, but then she said something to me which I have stored in my heart ever since. "How many of us know with certainty how many days we have left on this earth? Can any of us say that we will most definitely be alive in three years, or ten or forty?" She paused again and then quietly said, "If we are given the honor of becoming Zhen's new parents, we will love and treasure her every single day she has left on this earth."

I have never forgotten her words and the powerful wisdom contained in them. How many of us actually do know the number of days we have left to live? The number of days we have left to fulfill a dream or to mend fences with a loved one or to simply spend time with our kids? Through my work with children who are orphaned, I have learned so fully that it isn't a cliché to say that every day is important and an invaluable chance to make your time on this earth count. Life truly is a gift. Yet I still know that most of us are guilty of taking the days we are given for granted. It took a five-year-old little girl in a Chinese orphanage to help me realize that we need to cherish each and every day we are given together. Her wonderful new mom (yes, Zhen soon joined their family) showed me that adoption isn't about guarantees. It is about love, pure and simple, and the beauty that comes when you take a leap of faith and make a permanent commitment to a waiting child.

Six

Kui

As news of the successful heart surgeries in China started spreading, we began hearing from additional orphanages about children in need of medical help, which is how I ended up with the photo of a beautiful two-year old girl on my computer screen. Her name was Kui, from an orphanage in rural Guangxi Province. The facility was very poor, and they had been unable to raise the funds she needed for medical care. All they knew for certain was that she had some sort of heart issue as she tired easily and was very blue. At this point I was feeling pretty confident about helping her be seen at the hospital we had used for the other kids, and I would gaze often at her photo while making the arrangements and raising the funds needed. In the picture she was looking intently at the camera with her dark eyes, lying in a little metal bed with the now familiar blue lips of kids born with heart disease. I couldn't wait to see her turn a beautiful shade of pink.

We moved Kui to the hospital, and I was so happy and excited, thinking that helping children medically was the most wonderful thing in the world. She had a few extra tests run before surgery could be arranged, and then I got the startling news that the doctors felt Kui was inoperable. I couldn't even understand that word. Inoperable? If a child needs heart surgery, then you open them up and fix it, right? Surely something could be done to help Kui; she was only two years old after all. But I learned very quickly that the human body is a powerful thing, with an incredible determination to live.

When a child is born with heart disease and has to struggle to get enough oxygen because of it, his or her body will do anything possible to live another day. Unfortunately, the very things a body does to try and survive often lead to conditions that can prevent the heart from ever being healed surgically. We all probably learned in biology class that the aorta is the blood vessel that carries blood from our heart to arteries throughout the body, and blood travels from the heart back to the lungs for oxygen. This system is the very basis of life, and most of us don't think about it very often. But when a human body isn't getting enough oxygen, it will do whatever it takes to protect itself, sometimes forming a complex network of "collateral vessels" to the heart and lungs to reroute the way a heart functions. As our bodies adapt and rewire to divert blood and oxygen, it can cause an increase in pressure within our lungs' arteries, called pulmonary hypertension. When a child's body develops this condition, it often becomes chronic and permanent. It can then become impossible to perform surgery as the change in circulation would overwhelm the child's body, and she would quickly pass away following the operation.

Kui had extremely high pulmonary hypertension, along with extensive collateral vessels, and doctors told me that, at the incredibly young age of two, we were already too late to save her. I struggled to make sense of those words…TOO LATE. So we were supposed to do nothing? Just discharge her back to the orphanage to pass away? That seemed impossible to me in the age of modern medicine, and I couldn't comprehend those words because I was looking at the photo of a gorgeous little girl who deserved to get her fairy-tale ending. We had the funding in place to do her operation, and yet now I was being told that doing surgery would end her life almost instantly. Surely someone had made a mistake, and so her test results were sent for a second and third opinion. Each new doctor gave the same tragic news. There was nothing that could be done for Kui because we were simply too late. Her heart had needed to be repaired as an infant, and now nothing could be done to save her.

When we had learned that baby Kang might not make it post-surgery, I had to face the possibility of him dying as an orphan, and that was just unthinkable to me. Children are supposed to be with family. Children who are sick are supposed to have their moms and dads with them by their bedside, holding their hands and telling them they will be okay. Kids are supposed to have someone pacing the floor on their behalf, sending prayers to heaven and pleading with God to let their child live. They are not supposed to die on their own, and we certainly are not supposed to send them back to pass away in an orphanage. When I got the devastating news about Kui not having any chance at life, I had to do some serious soul-searching. I cried to God, asking what the purpose of a child's life was if she was only born into the world sick, to be abandoned by her parents, and then taken to an orphanage to die alone. Where is the purpose in that? What is the meaning of her even being born? None of my pleading questions changed the fact, however, that Kui would not be healed. There was no magic answer to that.

I sent a message to those who had given funds for her surgery, letting them know that Kui had been deemed inoperable. At the end of my emotional email, I asked that very question: Was Kui's life important? Just like when I would go to my mailbox and find letter after letter of people sending funds and prayers for baby Kang, my mailbox once again filled with notes written by people from all over the world. Each and every letter told me that Kui's life absolutely mattered. I received pictures and drawings from school children with "Kui is important" scrawled in crayon at the top. There were beautiful handwritten notes from grandmothers with blessings for little Kui, and cards and letters from parents who told me they wished that Kui could be with them so they could hold her and sing to her, even if only for a few days. My mailbox was filled with affirmation after affirmation that Kui's life was touching hearts and that she wasn't some unknown orphan on her own. People from around the world were thinking of her and sending their love.

Just a few short weeks after Kui was discharged from the hospital, I received the very sad news that she had quietly passed away. Her tiny body had finally given out. I hesitated to ask but needed to know... what would become of her body? In my heart I already knew the answer to the question, but I guess I just needed to hear it to affirm it was true. When a child dies in an orphanage, the tiny body is cremated, and there is no marker, no memory stone, no recognition that there was once a unique and perfectly wonderful child whose spirit had graced this earth. They are simply gone and probably too easily forgotten.

It was so hard for me to think of Kui dying before her beautiful baby photo could ever grace a parent's mantel. No school or graduation pictures of her would ever line the hallway of someone's home. I shared with a friend how much this pained my heart, to know that her life had disappeared before an adoptive family could someday bring her home and cherish her. She took my hand and reminded me that God has the biggest mantel in the world, with a photo of every single child we would ever try to save.

Since that time, through my work I have suffered through the loss of hundreds of beautiful children who were too sick to continue living. We now make memorial cards for each and every child who comes into our hands and leaves too soon, so that there will always be a record that they lived in our world and mattered to so many. But my favorite image still is of God's enormous mantel, stretching through the heavens, with the face of every beautiful child who has been born. Kui taught me that whether we are given just hours on this earth or an entire century, our lives can touch others in deep and lasting ways. She also made me realize that for many children in orphanage care, help can come too late if they don't get the medical treatment they need at the earliest possible time.

Seven

Unspeakable Need

By the summer of 2003, it was becoming very clear that the requests I was receiving to help orphaned children with surgery were not slowing at all. I had been contacted by several adoptive parents from my daughter's orphanage who wanted to go for themselves to meet the kids there, and I had also asked a close friend from church to consider going with me that summer as well. In early August, I met Donna Barthel and Shane Thompson for the first time at an airport gate in Chicago as we prepared to travel to China together. I liked them both immediately. Donna was a stay-at-home mom like me, with the kindest eyes and a ready laugh. Shane was an enormously tall R.N., which ended up being a source of much laughter for the people we met in China, as at that time they didn't have many male nurses. I still smile when I think about how many occasions he mentioned he was a nurse on that trip, and all of the officials would do a quick double take and say, "A nurse?," while shaking their heads in disbelief. Shane was such a wonderful sport, with a great sense of humor, even donning one of the little pink Chinese nursing hats at one point to pose for photos. Also in our group was my dear friend Nancy Delpha, who had agreed to join our team as well. After a brief conversation and telling each other about our families, the four of us boarded the plane to Hong Kong, anxious to meet many wonderful kids that week.

Each time I would return to China, I would learn things about orphanages that I hadn't known before. By this time I was making lots of new friends in both the adoption and charity worlds, and one of the hotly debated questions at that time was just how many orphanages actually existed in China. No one I asked could give me a definitive number. I was told that in 2003 about 250 orphanages had been approved for international adoptions. Many families had visited their children's facilities on adoption trips, and there were often photos of the institutions online, along with stories on family blogs about the conditions in many of them. With a simple Internet search, you could fairly quickly learn about the care in those places doing adoptions, but what about those facilities where foreigners had not been before? I had one official tell me there were 1,025 registered government orphanages in China, which would mean that 75% of orphanages at that time were not open to adoption or foreign visits. A professor in Beijing doing population studies told me he felt the number was more like 10,000 facilities caring for abandoned children when you added in the private ones, where local citizens were taking in babies found on the street and housing five to fifty children in often very sad conditions.

I was told very clearly, however, that foreigners were not supposed to visit the orphanages that didn't do international adoptions and so I shouldn't even ask if I could go to one. I will admit readily that I have always been a rule follower (which is why God probably decided to add some excitement to my life by giving me a few children who were not). I am always on time to appointments and don't cut in line. Most definitely when I heard that I wasn't allowed to visit any of these other facilities, I understood that I shouldn't ask. My heart was already broken for all of the children I had met in approved orphanages, simply because of the sheer number of kids needing homes, and so I told myself as we prepared for our trip to just let it go. However, once you hear there are places you aren't allowed to visit, it seems like it is human nature to start wondering more and more about them, even when unintended.

A few days after we landed in China, we got a phone call regarding an unregistered orphanage that wanted us to come visit. The man running the facility wanted support for the kids in his care and felt that if I could just see the conditions firsthand I would then be committed to helping them. We went back and forth on whether or not we should go and finally decided that we would make the long trip. We had to promise that we would bring no still or video cameras, and we were told to enter at the rear of the compound and then hurry inside immediately when the van dropped us off, so that no one would see that white people were in the area.

I am so ashamed now to admit that we were all very excited to make this trip. The whole "forbidden fruit" aspect was definitely going on. It took us many hours to get there; the whole way we were all laughing and joking with each other, having a grand old time, oblivious to what we were about to see. We pulled into the compound and then quickly hurried inside to a main upstairs room, where they brought in three terrified and visibly skinny children to be our greeters. They were absolutely petrified as they certainly had never seen a white person before. After a formal ceremony welcoming us to the orphanage, we were taken to the children's rooms. It pains me to even remember that the entire time we were in the meeting room upstairs, I was still thinking how GREAT it was that I had the opportunity to see a place that others had not.

The reality of children living in absolute and complete poverty soon washed over me, however. There are no adequate words to describe it, and I can't even bring myself to try and relive it completely as I have locked it away as a defense mechanism. All I allow myself are quick snips and pieces of images, quickly pushed away as I know it would be too painful to hold them for too long. I remember we walked into dark rooms with concrete walls covered in dirt. I remember a tiny rusted crib with five gaunt newborns lying side by side, all on their backs crying. I remember a three-year-old with a severe unrepaired cleft lip who began shrieking in terror when she saw me. To this day, if I pull up that memory, I can FEEL her sorrow in my head. The children were so thin, with the kind of vacant eyes that come when you have finally given up. There were children with no clothing, and children huddled in the corner. It was one of those situations that I cannot fully describe. You would have to have heard it and smelled it and felt it yourself to fully comprehend the absolute hopelessness of it all.

We were shaken to the core, and we didn't speak the entire way back to the hotel. We all came back to the United States as different people, and we all tried to deal with it in different ways. Donna told me that she wasn't even able to share the experience with her own husband, and when Nancy and I saw each other in person, we couldn't even look at each other without crying. I struggled at home with my family as well. I didn't want to make small talk with people at church or school. I didn't want to hear about their new cars or vacations, or pretend that everything was good. I was grieving with the harsh reality of what was happening to abandoned kids in our world, a reality that so many of us just have no idea about. This was a kind of impoverishment and hardship that I had only seen in occasional overseas news stories, but I had stood among the children in person and had seen the desperation and hunger on their faces with my own eyes. What had those children ever done to deserve that life? I was angry and confused and heartbroken.

The four of us talked many times by phone in the following weeks, wondering what in the world we could possibly do to make a difference as it just seemed too overwhelming. Too big. I couldn't bring myself to even go to church because I knew people would smile and say, "How was China?", expecting me to say, "Oh it was WONDERFUL." Instead I would drive out into the Oklahoma countryside and sit in my car, trying to come to terms with what I was supposed to do with what I had experienced that heartbreaking day. Of course, I knew life wasn't all about joy. I knew really bad things happened to people who didn't deserve them. People we love get cancer. Children are abused. Our world is filled with things the very opposite of joy and goodness. But what are we supposed to do with that knowledge? How are we supposed to keep going forward with hope when we find ourselves in situations which seem so completely overwhelming?

One Sunday, I drove out to a secluded spot and really began to pray. I told God that if it was His will, I would give my entire life to helping those who were orphaned. I would do whatever I could in my small way to help as many children as possible find healing. I cried a lot that morning as I sat there, and I didn't hear an answer back in my heart, but when I drove home later that day I felt more at peace than I had in weeks.

What happened next is one of those things that you look back on later and think, "Could that really have happened?" A few days later I got a knock on my door and a woman was standing there saying, "I know you're probably going to think I'm crazy, but I was praying today and had a message in my heart that I was supposed to come over and tell you that God accepts." Those were the exact words she told me: "God accepts." She had absolutely no idea what I had just pledged a few days before when I was out by myself in that field; yet here she stood on my doorstep telling me something she probably thought would make no sense to me. I'm sure I thanked her much too quickly while closing the door, and then, with my heart pounding, I realized I had to find a way to move past my own personal grief on what I had seen. The reality is that life isn't about 24-hour joy. It isn't always fair, or pretty, or just. There is very real sadness in our world. But what I realized that day is that when we see injustice or sorrow around us, even when it seems too big or immense to make a difference, we still have to try.

I picked up the phone and shared with Shane and Donna, my new friends from Indiana, what I thought God was asking me to do. I also called my friend Angela Carswell, an adoptive mom from North Carolina, and we talked for hours about what the next steps might be. I met with my friend Nancy, who thankfully lived close by, and we poured out our hearts to each other about what we felt we might be able to do to help the kids we had seen. A few days later we made the final decision to file incorporation papers to create a registered charity, dedicated to providing hope and healing to orphaned children. We took our name from a banner that had been presented to me by my daughter's orphanage following the first successful heart surgeries. It read, "Love Makes No Boundaries Between Countries," and so Love Without Boundaries was born. The five of us signed the legal documents to become the founding members of LWB. Truth be told, none of us at the time had any idea how to run a nonprofit. We just knew we wanted to help children. We were four moms and a nurse, but we pledged to each other that we would never forget those three little words which had been whispered to my heart: *Every child counts.*

On the day I dropped off the incorporation papers at the Oklahoma statehouse, I had no idea just how many children would someday come into our hands. I can say with complete certainty, however, that all these years later, those three words are still our driving principle. I am also happy to report that we went on to help many children in that impoverished orphanage we had visited with surgeries, essential supplies, and nutrition. A few years later, the local government in the city decided to provide them with a brand new building, and, when I visited the new facility several years ago, it could not have been more different than the concrete rooms I had seen in 2003. There was sunshine streaming through large windows, brightly colored murals adorned the hallways, and engaged children surrounded me. As I stood there holding a beautiful toddler we had helped with cleft surgery, I gave a silent prayer of thanks. My heart was reminded once again that when people come together in love, there can indeed be light from darkness and hope from despair.

Eight

The First Cleft Trip

There is a wonderful question frequently seen on motivational posters which says, "What would you attempt to do if you knew you couldn't fail?" That's definitely a good philosophical question to ask, but when I think back on the beginnings of LWB, I smile thinking of a slightly different question, "What did we attempt to do when we were completely oblivious to the difficulties?" Naiveté and a true lack of experience when it came to working in a foreign country were definitely components of our first year of projects in China. But to me, there can be a real beauty which occurs when you combine pure passion with simple innocence. Whereas those familiar with all the red tape that can come in working overseas might quickly state that a project is next to impossible to accomplish, those coming in unjaded still see the sky as the limit when it comes to helping those in need.

As word of our charity began to spread in Oklahoma, I was contacted by a local doctor who performed cleft lip repairs as part of his practice. He told me he had always wanted to help in China, and, if I could find a hospital willing to partner with us, he would assemble the entire medical team needed. I know I never would have attempted such an enormous project so soon as a newly founded charity, but here was a doctor promising to handle all of the major details if I could find a location open to a partnership. No matter that we knew nothing about the logistics of signing a contract with a Chinese hospital, and no matter that we knew nothing about securing foreign medical licenses or getting supplies through international customs, this sounded like a GREAT opportunity for the kids.

For unknown reasons, Asia has the highest incidence of cleft lip in the world, and I had seen so many children in Chinese orphanages with this unrepaired special need. I told the doctor we were definitely all in. What could be that hard anyway about planning an international medical mission? (Yes, that is my very poor attempt at sarcasm.) I flew to China in February of 2004 to meet with the director of the #2 Affiliated Hospital of Shantou University. This hospital was tied closely to the famous Hong Kong billionaire Li Ka Shing, whose foundation was doing amazing work helping impoverished people on the mainland with healthcare. The hospital I toured that day had state-of-the-art facilities, and our discussions about a possible medical exchange went very well. We agreed to partner together during the last week in May to provide surgery for approximately 50 to 60 orphaned children. We divided up who would be responsible for each part of the arrangement. The hospital would provide an entire ward for our patients, along with two operating rooms and nursing support. LWB would provide doctors and other medical staff, the list of patients, and any volunteers needed to keep the ward running smoothly.

My friend Dr. Huang, the doctor at the orphanage who had first taken me to baby Kang's crib the year before, told me that he would begin looking for children from orphanages throughout the province, and he felt very confident that we could quickly fill a busy surgery schedule. I left China later that week, honestly exhilarated thinking that things were going so smoothly.

I now know that when someone asks you if you are sitting down before delivering news, you probably want to find a chair. We were just eight weeks away from the cleft trip, and Dr. Huang had come through on his promise to identify kids needing surgery. I had information and photos on 55 children coming from 12 different orphanages, and every day I would sit and look at their photos, knowing that soon I would be meeting them all in person. We had raised all the funds we needed for the trip, and individual donors had been matched to the specific child they would be helping for surgery. But then came a call from the doctor leading the medical team, who unfortunately asked if I was sitting down. He went on to explain that he felt like he had been away from his family too much recently. He told me that meant he needed to back out of the trip, and, since it was all of his own medical staff who were going with us to China, he was going to have to pull them from the project as well. In the space of just a few minutes, the entire project had fallen apart. I hadn't been sitting when he called, but my heart sure began pounding about a million times a minute, and I don't even remember getting off the call.

I knew any second I was going to have a full-fledged emotional meltdown. In order to not terrify my kids, I quickly went out to my driveway and locked myself in my car. I know, I know… not a very original hiding spot, but it was all I could think of in my disbelief over what I had just been told. The faces of all of the kids we were planning to help were racing through my mind. How was I going to explain this to our friends in China who had worked so hard to identify the kids? How was I going to explain it to the hospital which had blocked that entire week for our team? And how were we going to tell each orphanage that the children we had promised to heal would not be receiving surgery? The enormity of having to "undo" what had already been planned in China washed over me, and I put my head on the steering wheel and began to pray.

I don't remember exactly what I said, but I know it went something like this: "God, there are 55 orphaned kids in China right now who need to have surgery, and we've already made a promise to their nannies that we will be there in two months. I know cleft trips take six months or more to plan, and I know doctors schedule their vacations sometimes a year in advance. But if there is any way at all to still help those children, I am just asking for the right people to find us because I have no idea where to even start. Please, if there is any way at all for those children to get the surgery they need... please send us a miracle."

The next morning, phone calls flew back and forth between our Board members as we agonized over what we should do. Should we cancel? Should we attempt to salvage the trip on our own? Where would we find doctors with just two months left when most mission trips are planned a year or more in advance? With each new phone call we had a different answer. It was off... it was on... the kids needed us... we couldn't handle this.

Later that afternoon, my phone rang and a warm, deep voice introduced himself as Dr. John Padilla, a plastic surgeon from Santa Barbara, California. He told me he had heard we were heading to China to do cleft surgeries, and he just wanted to call and offer his services on a future trip if we ever decided to go again. He said he had helped kids from Kosovo and Mexico and South America, but he had never had an opportunity to work in China. I took a deep breath and asked, "Any possibility you could go in eight weeks?" I remember him laughing, but, when he realized that I was actually being serious, he said, "Let me call you right back." Within an hour he had cleared his schedule and committed not only himself, but his OR team as well, all at his own expense. A few hours later, one of our Board members from North Carolina called and told me she had just confirmed with Dr. Lisa David, a cleft surgeon from Winston Salem, that she would be able to make the trip as well. Right about then I had goose bumps all over my arms, but it was soon to get even better.

I had posted news about the cleft surgery trip on several adoptive parent groups, and a few days later I received an email from Dr. Alan Reitz from Minnesota. He wrote that he was an adoptive dad from China himself, as well as being an anesthesiologist. Just like John Padilla had done, he offered his services on any trips in the future, and so, of course, I asked immediately if he could go in May. When he wrote back that he would be honored to be part of the team, you better believe I was lifting up prayers of thanks. After just a few more phone calls, we soon had all the nurses we needed as well. While I would never again want to try and pull together an entire medical team in the space of a few days, when it happened in 2004, it was glorious to watch unfold.

The new team of doctors was an absolute joy to work with. I can't even begin to tell you how many times I called them leading up to the trip with medical questions. The surgery group that had backed out had promised they would take care of all of the medical logistics of the trip, but now I found myself learning about international regulations and surgery planning in record time. Unfortunately, there was no "Medical Trips for Dummies" manual I could find online; so I would call Dr. Padilla and say, "What about customs?" "What about sterilization of instruments?" "What about sutures and retractors?" He would always kindly tell me it would all be okay and patiently explain what I needed to know.

In the blink of an eye, it was suddenly May. Since the team was flying in from locations all over the U.S., we decided to meet in Hong Kong first to introduce ourselves and plan for the upcoming week. Many of the volunteers on the team had never been to China before, and I was glad they had an extra day to rest up and get last minute cultural guidelines before we headed to the mainland. Every new team member I met was so nice and fun to be around, and I could tell within hours that it was going to be an amazing week. Our hotel floor was a whir of activity as it all started to hit us that the very next day the medical part of the trip would begin.

We had a six-hour bus ride from Hong Kong to Shantou, with over 40 large suitcases filled with medical instruments, surgical supplies, sutures, and medications. Dr. Padilla had told me several times by phone that he would handle everything with customs since he done international trips before. As we got closer to the border of the mainland, I asked him if he had the forms we would need and what I could do to help out. He gave me a huge smile and told me that his plan was just to be as nice as he could possibly be to the customs agents, and he was sure it would all work out fine. At first I thought he was kidding with me, especially since we were traveling with such extensive medical equipment, but then I quickly realized this had been his plan all along. He shared with me the great quote about it being far easier in many cases to ask for forgiveness than permission. I am sure my face must have fallen in panic because he clapped me on the back and told me not to worry, singing a bit of Bob Marley's "Everything's Gonna be Alright." You know how some people will hold their breath when they drive by a cemetery for good luck? Well, I think I held my breath through the entire customs crossing. Thankfully, John's warm explanation to the border agents about how many orphaned children we were going to help was more than enough to get the official approvals we needed, and we soon found ourselves arriving in Shantou, where the local government had hung an enormous red banner to welcome our team. The city orphanage had offered their building as the evaluation area for the doctors, and, when we pulled into the courtyard as far as I could see were nannies holding babies and children with cleft needs. It seemed like each orphanage had tried to outdo the other by dressing their kids in new outfits to wish them good luck on their journey.

We stepped out to a sea of waiting children, and it was wonderful to recognize the babies and kids I had only known before through photographs. Now came the most difficult part of any type of medical trip: deciding which babies would receive surgery and which ones would not qualify. Dr. Reitz, who remains to this day one of the most incredible doctors I have ever worked with, explained to me that with cleft surgery most doctors follow a rule of 10-10-10. The first ten signifies that each child must be ten weeks old to undergo anesthesia. Thankfully all of the children waiting in the courtyard met that requirement. The second ten requires that kids have a hemoglobin level of ten on their blood work, which is the protein in red blood cells that carries oxygen throughout the body. When this number drops too low, people develop anemia and are much more likely to have serious complications before and after surgery. Unfortunately, many orphaned children have low hemoglobin levels as their diets are often very low in protein and iron; so it is not uncommon for a child from an orphanage to be below ten. The final ten stood for the minimum weight requirement needed for surgery. Dr. Reitz explained that any baby approved by the team would need to weigh at least ten pounds in order to undergo their operation. While that seems like it would be an easy feat for any child of at least three months old, babies in orphanages often struggle to gain the weight. Sadly, that day several babies did not make weight, and I saw more than one nanny begin to cry when learning the news.

There was one baby girl that day who particularly concerned our team as we learned she was from an orphanage with very limited resources in a much more rural part of the province. Her paperwork stated that she was almost nine months old, but on the intake day she weighed just seven pounds. Babies with cleft lip and palate often struggle to eat as they are unable to form the suction needed to pull milk from a bottle's nipple. In orphanages with limited caregivers, babies are often "prop fed," meaning that a towel or small blanket is placed next to them, and the bottle is then propped for them to somehow eat on their own versus being hand fed. This is a less than ideal way for any infant to eat, of course, but for babies with cleft, they often fail to get the nourishment they need to grow and thrive since they can't form a good seal with the bottle. This was obviously the case for little Peanut, as she came to be known that week. She was painfully thin and clearly failing to thrive, falling far short of the ten pound weight requirement. Her skin was extremely pale, and she had many dark red bug bites on her tiny face. I know many of our team members tried their best not to cry when looking at her fragile state. Instead of just sending her immediately back to her orphanage, however, we asked if she could stay for the week in Shantou so the medical team could better decide whether it would be safe to do her operation. I know we were all grateful when her orphanage agreed.

It was difficult to compare tiny Peanut, who looked so weak and gaunt that day, with the two babies our team evaluated next. LWB had recently begun working with the New Hope Foundation, a wonderful charity based outside of Beijing. Dr. Joyce and Robin Hill ran the Hope Foster Home there and had devoted their lives to taking in abandoned babies with medical needs. At their wonderful facility, orphaned babies received all the TLC and nurturing they required to be restored to health. Dr. Hill had called us a few weeks before about twin baby girls she was caring for at their center, who had been born with mirror image clefts. She asked if they could possibly receive surgery from our team in Shantou, and we gladly agreed to make room on the schedule. On evaluation day, the twins were the very picture of health, with chubby cheeks and arm rolls. When they had first arrived to the Hills' care, however, they too were underweight and in a very vulnerable state. They had been left at the gate of a local orphanage, with a note from their birth mom saying she was unable to care for them. Their tiny size when found was a clear indication they had struggled to feed as well. Thankfully, at the Hope Foster Home they had access to special cleft bottles for the nannies to use to squeeze milk into a baby's mouth. The difference these bottles can make in the life of a child with cleft was so obvious to our team as we looked at the stark contrast between the twins who benefited from them compared to the majority of kids that day from orphanage care.

The next morning was the official opening of the cleft trip at the hospital. The U.S. and Chinese medical teams all met for the first time on the surgery ward. I will admit it was a very chaotic beginning as we tried to figure out in two different languages the final schedule and who would work together in each operating room. The room seemed to get louder and louder as more people shared their opinions, and then I watched Dr. Padilla look around and suddenly smile. He walked over to a hospital bed and picked up one of the Hope Foster Home twins. He looked at me and winked and said, "Okay, let's go." He then disappeared down the hallway with the baby in his arms, walking calmly through the OR room doors. That was all the encouragement we needed. We took a deep breath and hurried after him, knowing it was time to begin. Within just a few hours, our newly formed international medical team had found its rhythm, and it was extraordinary to watch each new baby come out of surgery transformed.

By the end of that incredible week, over 50 babies and children had been healed. It was getting late in the afternoon on the final operating day when Dr. Padilla gathered the team together to discuss baby Peanut. I have a photo on my computer from that day of John holding this little girl, and she looks like a tiny rag doll in his arms. The reality of any international medical trip is that no one wants to take unnecessary risks. As guests of a foreign country, we didn't want to cause problems for either side, and, of course, to have a child die from complications in surgery would be a horrible tragedy none of us wanted to imagine. While both medical teams wanted every child to be healed that week, we also wanted to do the operations safely, and Peanut had missed the 10-10-10 mark. In most situations like this, we would send the child back to the orphanage, promising to arrange surgery once the child reached the needed weight. But it was obvious that Peanut was failing quickly, and Dr. Padilla said that he felt in his heart that she would have a much better chance at taking a bottle if he could close her wide cleft lip. I know the local doctors weren't completely convinced as they felt she was just too sick and tiny to undergo an operation. I will never forget John putting his hand on his Chinese colleague's shoulder and saying, "This is a human life, and we have to try." So Peanut became the 53rd child on that trip to go into surgery, looking so incredibly tiny on the operating room table. With much joy, I can say that she came through the procedure beautifully, and the best part of all is that she began to thrive after she was able to eat properly for the first time. Her orphanage let us know just one month later that she had already gained over two additional pounds. I know without a doubt that Dr. Padilla saved not only her smile that day in Shantou, but her precious life as well.

On the bus ride back to Hong Kong when our surgery week had ended, Dr. Padilla made a promise to me that he would travel every year with LWB to China. He said the trip had impacted him in ways he had never imagined. We were sitting one bus seat away from each other, and he leaned back suddenly and said, "Tell me what you are dreaming about with LWB, Amy. What do you want to see happen in the future?" After the absolutely exhausting week we had just been through, I know I gave some completely lame answer about doing more surgeries and helping more kids, which he thankfully challenged immediately. He started brainstorming and asking question after question about what we could create together if we dared to envision it. "What if we could form a cleft center in China to provide free medical care so that parents would never have to make the agonizing decision to abandon their child born with cleft?" "What if we figured out a way to train caregivers in orphanages about how to better feed these kids?" Again and again on that six-hour ride he would say, "What if we tried this?" or, "Have you ever thought of that?" I kept saying, "John, you have to realize we're just a small charity, and we're only getting started." He would smile that incredible smile of his and say, "Amy, dream big, dream big, dream big."

I really thought that perhaps Dr. Padilla would return back to his busy practice in the U.S. and forget about the orphaned children he had met in China, but I should have known better. He checked in with me regularly about planning the next cleft trip, and he told me he was making inquiries with his connections in the medical world as to how we could more easily provide care for the kids. I talked with him at the beginning of November to ask him about dates for a 2005 trip, but just a few weeks later I answered the phone to hear unthinkable news. Dr. Padilla had been killed in a small plane crash in California at the far too young age of 50. It was impossible to believe that a man with such a gift for helping others had been taken from the world too soon.

I flew to California to attend his funeral and realized while I was there that I had never told him the story about praying for a miracle that day in my driveway. I sure wish I had because I know God had connected us for a reason. To have been sent the gift of his surgical abilities would have been miracle enough to me. But to have been sent the gift of him as a person was a blessing I will carry with me forever. John lived believing that the only real failure in life comes from not trying. "Dream big, dream big, dream big." I will never forget his words. He showed me so clearly that when we give from our hearts and take risks for children in need, we can change lives in the most amazing ways.

Nine

The First School

LWB's relationship with my daughter's orphanage continued to strengthen, and on my trips there I fell more in love each time with the children who called the welfare institute home. It was a very unusual orphanage because many of the staff members were related to each other, and so it had much more of a family feel to it than other facilities I visited. The nannies and staff would often take kids home with them on the weekends, and it was clear that it wasn't a lack of love that was stopping them from making improvements to care but simply a lack of funding.

On each visit I would get to know the children who lived there better, learning the wonderful nicknames the nannies had given them, such as Little Goose, White Piggy, and even Beefball (named after the local delicacy as they said she was so cute they could just eat her up). By then the kids knew that when I visited there would be lots of treats, including their favorite Kix cereal, which the nannies hadn't seen before but which they happily handed out when I told them they were "secret vitamin balls." Each doorway of the orphanage had a shiny metal gate halfway up to keep the kids in their intended rooms. As I would walk down the hallway, the children would grasp the bars tightly and call, "Ayi! Ayi!" to get my attention, with the hope I would stop and hand them another yummy snack. I will never forget the day that a beautiful little girl named YuHan was the first to figure out she could scale the gate to freedom. Once she was up and over, the others stood there for a second in disbelief, and then, like little lemmings, they all climbed over to dash down the hallway after me, shrieking with delight. I don't think the orphanage ever fully kept them contained after that. One night, when I was in the intake room late at night looking at a newborn just admitted who needed medical care, I suddenly felt a little hand tugging on my pants. It was YuHan once again, grinning up at me way past her bedtime, with two of her friends standing beside her. They had stealthily climbed over the gate of their room to explore the dark hallways while others slept. I could only smile at the little adventurers, and Dr. Huang put his finger to his lips to tell them to be quiet before giving them a snack and leading them back to their beds. I wonder how many other nights they made that secret run.

Another of the preschool-aged children who quickly stole my heart was little Mei. She was nonstop energy and stuck to me like Velcro. As soon as I would arrive in the morning, she would stretch out her arms for me to pick her up, and woe to the child who tried to take her spot on my hip while I carried her around as she would give them an emphatic swat to their heads. She was such a smart little girl and listened carefully to my English words so she could repeat them again and again. One day, I walked into her room and she loudly called out "Mama!" before running over to grab my legs. "Up, up, up," she would say. When I would lift her to my body, she would wrap her little legs around my waist and hold onto me tightly. These were the moments which hurt my heart so deeply as all of the kids in the orphanage deserved to have families of their own. They just soaked up every single second I would hug them or hold them on my lap. I'll never forget the day that I was leaving the orphanage after being there for over a week. Someone must have told Mei that I was going to the van because she streaked like lightning down the steps yelling, "Wait for me. Wait! I need my shoes!" She jumped up into my arms in the courtyard saying, "We can go now." When she realized I wasn't going to take her with me, she began to sob, and it pierced me to the core to have to literally peel her off of me and hand her struggling and fighting to a nanny. As the van pulled away to take me to the airport, I could hear her loudly crying out, "Mama! Mama!" It felt like such a betrayal to love on these kids so completely for a week only to leave them behind to head back to my life at home.

Then there was YaYa, an adorable three-year-old with little apple cheeks, who had been born with a medical need which at the time deemed her as unadoptable from China. She had watched somberly as several of her best friends were chosen by families and left the orphanage, of course, not understanding that her paperwork wasn't able to be filed. A visitor to the orphanage had given YaYa a beautiful red quilted coat, which she loved with all her heart. She wore it nonstop and never wanted to take it off as it was something given just to her, which is such a rarity in orphanage care. When the orphanage staff had decided to send me information on the first three kids needing heart surgery, they had taken YaYa's red coat off of her to put on the "little blue girl." They wanted Zhen to have something beautiful to wear in her photo since doctors in America would see it. When her coat was taken from her, YaYa began to cry loudly. Everyone could hear her sobbing from outside the room.

As Zhen was having her photos taken in the hallway, YaYa ran to the metal gate at the door and cried some more. The aunties tried to move her back into the room, but she used all of her strength to hang onto the gate tightly while crying. The nannies actually scolded her and said, "YaYa, you must share your red coat. You cannot be selfish." But still she continued to cry. Finally one of the nannies listened to what she was saying and realized YaYa wasn't crying because she didn't want to share. She was crying because she wanted her photo taken as well. She said over and over, "Take MY photo. Please take my picture too!" You see, she had already realized at the tender age of three that in order to have a mom and dad come to take you home, you first had to have your picture taken. She thought they were taking Zhen's photo so that Zhen could be chosen for adoption. YaYa wasn't crying because she didn't want to share her coat with her friend; she was crying because she wanted a family of her very own and felt it might never happen. These were just some of the kids I now carried deeply in my heart. How I wished I could give them everything possible.

In China, education is prized above all else for a child, and families often compete for the best schools for their kids. It is not uncommon for even toddlers in wealthier families to go to private boarding kindergartens. I had visited several on my overseas trips, and I would watch kids as young as 20 months bravely walk in and tell their moms goodbye. Tiny wooden toddler beds would line the walls, and the kids would live there until their parents would come back to take them home for holidays. The Shantou orphanage staff was very proactive in trying to have the kids in their care have the best opportunities possible. They had found a small boarding school in the city that finally agreed to let some of the children attend as "charity cases." They offered the orphanage five spots. Zhen and Qiang (who had heart surgery the year before), Mei, and two others went to live at the school. That first week, however, did not go well. The principal called and said the kids were all crying and unhappy. The same thing happened the next week and the next. A month after the kids had started, Dr. Huang and I visited the children, and they ran into his arms and began sobbing once more, begging him to please let them return to the orphanage. They told Dr. Huang how miserable they were at school because of the constant teasing by other kids since they were orphans, from the staff who didn't want to go near them because of their "unlucky" special needs, and from the parents who were rude and unkind to them, saying their bad fortune and "cursed spirits" could rub off on their own children. It was my first experience seeing the enormous stigma which can follow a child who is orphaned in China. As we took the kids back to the orphanage, Dr. Huang sighed heavily. On the one hand, he knew the kids needed to be in kindergarten if they were going to have any chance of getting on a proper track for education. But on the other hand, he definitely didn't want to destroy the children's emotions and self-esteem by having them be told again and again they were outcasts because of their orphan status.

We talked at length about how many other kids in the orphanage had medical needs which completely prevented them from ever attending public school – kids who were deaf or blind; kids with cerebral palsy or limb differences; and kids with needs such as Down Syndrome, albinism, or incontinence. These children would not be allowed to attend public schools because parents would vocally disapprove of their kids being taught alongside them, and school officials wouldn't accept the liability of having children with medical issues enrolled. For many of the kids in orphanages, outside school simply wasn't an option. It was far too common for children with special needs to instead spend their days in beds or in chairs, often becoming withdrawn and definitely not realizing their wonderful potential. Then Dr. Huang said the words that launched LWB's next program area: "If these kids can't go to school, it's too bad that school can't come to them."

Yes, it was a light bulb moment for us. Why couldn't school come to them? Could we set up in-orphanage classrooms so that all of the kids could experience the joy of learning? We walked up the stairs to look at three big rooms which were used mainly for storage, and I was already imagining a play room with dress-up clothes and building blocks, and classrooms with chalkboards and brightly colored desks. Just like with the cleft trip, none of us had any idea how to set up a project this big, but since we knew there were over 40 older kids in the orphanage needing it to happen, we were determined to make it a reality.

Within just a few months, we had been blessed to raise all the funds needed for the start up, and I soon found myself back in Shantou to help convert the storage rooms into our very first school. We had ordered 30 sets of tables and chairs from IKEA at the amazing price of $8 each, which, of course, arrived needing to be assembled. We spent an entire day putting them together. As they began piling up, I could tell that the unfinished wood color wasn't going to give the colorful effect I had been hoping for. I will plead the fifth on coming up with the brilliant idea that perhaps each child could paint an individual chair and desk in order to give them ownership of their personal workspace. This didn't seem to translate very well to the nannies, who were frantically trying to tell me the kids couldn't participate, but back then I still hadn't mastered the Eastern versus Western way of doing things. Very reluctantly, they brought the children out to the main activity room, where multiple paint colors were brought in as well. I'll just say that about ten minutes in, I realized I hadn't thought this through very well as we had no drop cloths or paint smocks, and the kids had never even seen a crayon, much less a huge can of paint and their own paintbrush. I am sure you can imagine the scene as dozens of exuberant kids splashed, poured, and splattered paint from one end of the room to the other. And, of course, when you mix red, blue, and yellow paints all together (a concept not yet taught to the kids since school hadn't opened yet), I watched as the tables and chairs starting turning an odd shade of mud. Yes, it was chaos, and yes we ended up having to retile the activity room floor when the director came in and realized the room where he held official gatherings now looked like a Jackson Pollock painting. Whoops. But it was the kids' first lesson, albeit a messy one, that we truly valued their creativity and efforts.

Once the classrooms were set up, it was time to hire our very first teachers. With the number of private schools in the city expanding rapidly, our ad to recruit teachers to work inside an orphanage honestly didn't result in many applicants. The first three women we hired actually quit within days on the job. One said the noise of babies crying in other rooms was too much for her to take, while another was much blunter, stomping out of the orphanage on her very first day saying the facility was terrifying and the children were scary. Losing three teachers within the first week was very disheartening to us all, and we met again to discuss what our actual goal was for the very first school. Did we really need teachers with four-year university degrees? Or were we hoping instead for teachers who would love and accept the kids for exactly who they were? The answer to that question was pretty obvious of course; so we began advertising at junior vocational schools to try and find grads open to taking on this new challenge.

Within a few weeks, we had two young ladies apply for the positions. They came to the orphanage with their freshly received preschool teaching certificates in hand, and we quickly learned that they were both just 18 years old. At first I balked at their very young age, but they were so gentle with the kids, picking them up and giving them hugs, and they didn't seem to be phased at all by those with special needs such as cleft lip or a missing hand. When Dr. Huang said it was clear that they honestly enjoyed being with the children, that was all we needed to know. They were the ones. At that time in China, new teachers from vocational schools were paid just 800 rmb a month (about $100 USD), but the reality is that these two ladies were worth far more than gold and diamonds. Their hearts were so kind and loving, and they excitedly went up to Beijing to get additional Montessori training as we felt that letting each child work at his or her own pace was the exact model we wanted. Soon after, the doors to our very first "Believe in Me" school opened. We chose this name because we knew that so many of the children had been judged as "lacking" due to their special needs, and it was our hope to spread the message that every child born has immeasurable worth and deserves a chance to learn and people to believe in them.

Soon the walls of the orphanage were filled with children's artwork, and the kids began learning poems and stories. On my next visit back, one of my favorite moments was when the very first Believe in Me choir put on a performance for me to watch. Mei, YuHan, and Zhen were all holding hands as they loudly sang about a white rabbit with two ears. At the head of the choir was a young boy with Down Syndrome, who up until the school had opened had spent his days sitting in a single room all day staring at the walls around him. I watched as he waved a little wand in the air and kept perfect time to the music. He turned to me when the song was over and gave me the hugest grin. The perfect conductor, glowing with pride at his newly given responsibility.

To say that this school changed those children's lives is an understatement. The orphanage, which you might remember had been much too quiet the year before, was now filled with the sounds of laughter and singing. The other wonderful thing about the school is that as the kids came out of their "institutional blankness," more and more of them were given the chance to have their adoption paperwork filed.

There was one little girl named Ting, who had spina bifida as a baby which had left her with some long term medical issues. She was six years old, and when I would visit, she would always be sitting in the corner on a stool for hours and hours at a time. It always made me quite sad as the other kids would come and jump on me, but Ting would sit "planted" in the corner, looking solemnly at me and never joining in because she had been told she wasn't able to get up and walk around. When our school opened its doors, the teachers were so amazing with her. They included her in all the activities and kept coming up with ways she could stay longer in the classroom with them. Within months she was like a different child. Later I always tried to get her to laugh when I visited because I had discovered she had this wonderful giggle which was so soft and low.

Over the years, Ting had watched baby after baby be adopted. Sometimes the new families would make the journey to visit the orphanage, and Ting would watch them proudly holding their new child while saying they were the luckiest parents in the world. But because of her special need and because she had been so very solemn and withdrawn before, the orphanage had never considered filing her adoption paperwork. Attending our school had finally allowed her to bloom. One day she and I were sitting together at her desk, and the teacher told me how much she was progressing each day. She was coloring a picture and would stop to answer the questions I asked, such as her favorite subject, her favorite color, and what she liked to eat best. At the end of our talk, I asked her if there was anything I could ever bring her when I visited. Shyly, Ting nodded her head yes. With a quiet voice she looked up at me and said, "Please, I would like a mama of my own."

With a lump in my throat, I took Ting's hand and promised her that I would do everything in my power to help her find a family, and I was so grateful when the orphanage agreed that she should have that chance. Just a few months later, a wonderful family stepped forward and said they wanted to bring her home. I gave the orphanage the happy news, and they immediately told Ting that a family was coming for her. While the family in the U.S. gathered papers and permissions from the government, Ting waited in excitement. While the family sent off their completed paperwork and prepared their house for a new daughter, Ting waited some more. Over and over she asked, "When is my mom coming? When is the day?", and the orphanage staff would say, "Soon, soon." But when you have been waiting six years for a family to choose you, waiting even one more day is very hard indeed. Finally, Ting's new mom and dad arrived in China, completing all of the legalities before boarding their plane with their new daughter to head back to the U.S. As Ting excitedly said goodbye to those who had cared for her, she kept saying, "Wo hen gaoxing, wo hen gaoxing, mama baba." One of the nannies who spoke English asked the parents if they knew what she was saying, and they shook their heads no. She told them, "She is saying, 'I'm so happy, I'm so happy. I have a mom and a dad.'" The quiet wish Ting had told me that day in the classroom had finally come true for her.

Since the day we opened the doors of our first Believe in Me school, hundreds of children just like Ting have had their own chance to blossom and shine. The kids in our schools love class time so much that when it is time for a holiday they will often barricade the school room door and beg the teachers not to leave. That is such a far cry from my own kids counting down the days until school will get out. For children in institutional care, however, having the opportunity to learn, create, and explore is such a true gift. I'm so thankful that Dr. Huang asked that question all those years ago of whether we could bring school to the kids. We have since opened classrooms in nine Chinese provinces, and children from our education program now live in countries around the world. Wo hen gaoxing. Wo hen gaoxing. I'm so happy. I'm so happy.

The Heart of an Orphan

Ten

Foster Care

Up until this point, all of the projects we had done in China were for children living inside social welfare facilities. We had bought hundreds of safe cribs and thousands of warm blankets for children in orphanages in over a dozen Chinese provinces. We had provided life-changing surgeries and, in fact, became the very first foreign foundation to support the national government's new Tomorrow Plan, an incredibly ambitious project to provide medical care to orphaned children needing surgery. LWB donated the very first overseas funds to the Tomorrow Plan, and eight children born with congenital heart defects were the first ones healed through that now very successful program. But all of our support so far had been for children living inside an institution's walls.

I had become an avid reader of anything involving orphan care, and I quickly learned that many researchers felt that, for every three months spent in an institution, a child loses an average of one month of growth. I had, of course, seen that with my own daughter, who had been handed to me weighing just ten pounds at almost a year of age. She had such little muscle tone that, when we would try to sit her up on the floor, she would just sink to the side like a limp noodle. As we would visit orphanages where the kids spent the majority of time in their cribs, we saw children who were clearly delayed, with few meeting the standard developmental milestones for their ages. Again and again we would wish they could get the 1:1 care they deserved. Children need parents – it isn't rocket science. So our Board began discussing whether LWB should begin its first foster care project.

Okay, I will admit now that I was terrified of taking this on. As I just mentioned, up to this point all of our projects had been either one-time gifts, like supplies or a surgery, or else our single school project in Shantou where we provided care for the kids during the day, but then they went back to their nannies in the evening. To me, foster care would be a game-changer for LWB as we would actually be taking kids from an institutional setting and placing them into local homes in the community. We would be giving orphaned children their very own FAMILY – the most precious gift a child can receive – and that meant we would be making a full-time commitment. We couldn't start and then change our minds and take that safety and security away from them, and we couldn't start a project like this and then decide we were done being a charity. Foster care was a long-term promise to a child so that they could bond and attach to their very own mom and dad, and LWB would be there to provide the resources necessary to keep that family unit intact. Insert giant gulp of panic here.

Two things came together which finally convinced me we needed to take this important next step. First, I got an email from a woman in the U.K. named Arlene Howard asking if it would be possible for LWB to visit her daughter's orphanage to see what needs they might have. Yes, I will admit in my dorkiness I thought getting an email from someone in England was pretty darn exciting. I had never met anyone from that country before, and I may or may not have tried reading the email in a bad British accent before writing her back that we would love to help. Her daughter's orphanage was in Anhui, an Eastern farming province on the Yangtze River, and one we had not visited before.

I look at photos from that first trip to Dingyuan now and give thanks that the orphanage was so open to partnering with us to better the lives of the children in their care. The majority of kids we met had been born with special needs. Many of the nannies were actually afraid to let the children in their care exert themselves, and so the children with cerebral palsy, heart issues, or other medical conditions were lying flat on their backs in the cribs, bundled so tightly with blankets that they could barely even move. We were told again and again, "We are afraid they will hurt themselves," when we would ask why the kids weren't allowed to be up and about. The children stared up at us with solemn eyes, and it was clear that they were greatly delayed. We knew they wouldn't be able to progress as long as their only view of the world was the ceiling, and so I finally gave in to the rest of our Board, who had understood far sooner than me that orphaned children need families supporting them. Every child needs a dedicated caregiver to nurture and encourage their steps forward.

At around the same time, we received an email from Kim Burghart. She was a mom from Kansas who had adopted a baby girl named Marissa from an orphanage in southern China many years before. Tragically, at the age of eight, she had been taken from this world after bravely battling a malignant brain tumor. I had followed their story online and had prayed many times for this beautiful little girl who loved the color purple, horses, and creating art. Her mom wrote that she wanted somehow to use the drawings Marissa had made while she battled cancer to help other children in need. She told us that her daughter cherished having a family more than anything else in the world, and she wondered if we could perhaps use her artwork to raise funds which would allow even more kids to have homes.

That was just the encouragement we needed to sign our first foster care contract with the Dingyuan orphanage. We agreed to begin the program with ten children being placed in families in a wonderful close-knit community of single-story row houses. There were lots of discussions back and forth on what rules we wanted in place for LWB foster care. One of the lengthiest debates came over how many children we would allow in a single home. I myself was parenting six kids at the time, as was Board member Donna Barthel, and so it felt a little strange to insist that a family could have no more than two children in the home. But we all agreed that we wanted the kids we moved out of orphanage care to have as much individual time with their new parents as possible. We also knew that with the one-child policy in China, we didn't want to bring too much attention to our foster parents by having them go to the market or the park with a long row of little ducks following after them. We talked extensively about the health checks we wanted each family member to get, including exams for Hepatitis B and tuberculosis, along with immunizations if they hadn't received them before.

In the U.S., if you mention "foster care," many people immediately think of a broken system. We read of kids being shuttled from one home to the next with reports of far too many children experiencing abuse or neglect. With one quick Internet search you are faced with article after article about an overburdened American foster care program with a history of leading children to homelessness, depression, and incarceration. In fact, the company we were using for our liability insurance told me that they could not continue covering us if we added foster care in China to our programs. It was quite simply a deal breaker for many companies. But we knew the research showed again and again that orphaned children needed homes, not institutions, and so we continued moving forward with our plans. We felt that the key to successful foster care was to make sure the families had both the financial and emotional support they needed. We were asking them to take care of children with special needs which were often looked down upon in China; so the wages had to be fair and the families needed to know we would be there for them when questions and concerns came up. At the time, there were several other charities providing foster care in China, and I had sponsored children through some of them in the past. I knew that because of the remote regions of some of the foster care villages, the charity staff could only visit quarterly or sometimes even just once per year. We were worried that could be too long between visits as we wanted to be able to quickly know if a child wasn't thriving or meeting milestones. We decided that each time we opened a foster care location, we would find a local person living in the same city who could visit the families every single month. I am convinced that having these wonderful local managers is what has allowed us to so dramatically change countless lives through home care. Our managers form close bonds with the families, and the foster parents know they can pick up the phone and call our staff at any time if they are worried about a child getting sick or if they need additional nutrition or other services.

We have since gone on to open foster care in over 20 regions of China. When I say that foster care is one of my absolute most favorite programs, I mean that with all my heart. I have been blessed again and again to spend time with our amazing foster moms, like Granny Wei, who answered our ad for foster parents by pedaling her tricycle over three miles to the orphanage. When the orphanage director said he felt she might be a bit too old in her 70s to care for a baby, she pedaled back home that night and sewed a complete layette set, pedaling back the next morning to ask once more if she could share her love for children with a baby in need. The orphanage director knew this determined grandmother wasn't going to give up, and she soon was given a failure-to-thrive baby boy named Fei to care for. Granny Wei lived all by herself, and so she had every moment of the day to devote to this little boy. We watched him gain much needed weight that first month, and then he doubled his size by the third. She kept pedaling back to the orphanage with Fei sitting beside her in a little basket to request additional cans of Nestle formula, and we finally had to tell her that the baby really didn't need to eat every hour on the hour as he had developed not a double, but triple chin!

I also smile when I think of visiting Xiang's wonderful foster mom and the store-bought coat I had brought him for the upcoming winter. It was a typical ski type jacket, and I was excited to hand her the new coat for the little boy she was caring for. She tried her very best to be polite, but finally she couldn't help herself and had to go get the padded coat and pants she had been making by hand all summer for him. It felt 100 times warmer than the coat I had just handed her, and I started laughing when she told me quite bluntly, "Mine's better." I completely agreed! She loved that little boy so much, and it showed in each of the thousands of tiny embroidered stitches in the quilted coat she had made just for him. A literal cloak of love, which is what every child on earth deserves to be wrapped in. I have to admit that on one of my visit's to Xiang's home, I panicked when I learned that the foster father had moved out of the house. I asked the foster mom what had happened, and she explained that she insisted on having the little boy sleep in her bed so that he would feel safe and secure at night. She said that her husband complained mightily about constantly being kicked all night long by Xiang, and he finally announced he would now be sleeping at his parents' house nearby. I was speechless for a few moments, thinking that LWB foster care had somehow broken up a marriage, and somehow managed to mumble out an apology to the foster mom for causing any issues with their relationship. She started laughing loudly and clapped me on my knee, saying with glee, "It's okay lady, I like the baby much more than the husband!"

I know that when people think of life-saving programs, they almost always think of medical care first and foremost. But as we began placing more and more children into home care, it became clear that foster care can also literally save a child's life. For children born with cleft lip, for example, who truly need to be hand fed, having their very own mom or dad hold them while patiently squeezing milk into their mouths, can drastically cut mortality. I have seen the same result for babies prone to other medical conditions as well. We had begun working with an orphanage many years ago in a truly impoverished region of China hit very hard by the blood selling tragedy in the 1990s. During that time, in order to bolster China's plasma supply, collection agents would pay villagers to come and give blood, which was then pooled without testing for HIV or Hepatitis. Once the plasma was removed, the blood would be re-injected into those who had sold it, sadly transmitting illness to an estimated 100,000 people. The small rural village where the orphanage was located had been greatly impacted by disease, and many of the rural farmers were struggling to survive. When there aren't enough resources for the local families to get by, the funds for those who are orphaned are even scarcer.

The first time we visited this orphanage, we were taken to a crumbling building which didn't even have the funds to put glass in the windows or to hang wooden doors. The baby rooms opened directly to the outside courtyard, even though this region gets very cold in the winter with snow. The orphanage didn't have any sort of heating system either, and the price of coal to warm the entire large building was well beyond their reach. To add insult to injury, the director explained that the over 100-year-old building was in the middle of a flood plain. Every spring, the rooms where the children lived would fill with river water. While we did our best over the next year to do what we could to improve their living conditions, we realized that one clear solution for the babies in this orphanage was to get them moved into family care, especially for those with medical needs which made them prone to respiratory infection. The orphanage director told us that they lost many babies each winter when they became sick, and I honestly at the time didn't realize just how many babies around the world succumb to pneumonia each year. It is the leading cause of childhood mortality around the globe, claiming over a million young lives annually. When we began moving the children from this damp orphanage out into local homes, the director told us with gratitude that more and more children were surviving each year.

We saw such remarkable progress being made by the kids we moved into home care that LWB set a goal to open as many foster care programs as we could financially sustain. One brisk autumn day, I found myself walking through the streets of a small city in Hunan Province. At the time, the one-child policy was still firmly in effect, and especially so in this province, which was the birthplace of Chairman Mao. We would always gather a large crowd around us as we did our foster care visits as foreigners weren't commonly seen in these more out-of-the-way towns, and especially not going in and out of local homes. As we came out of the final apartment, the foster parents walked out with us, one holding a baby and the other a squirming toddler. The crowd pressed closer, and one man shouted out, "Why is this family allowed to have two children?" The orphanage director was with us, and she began explaining to the crowd that we had recently set up a foster care program in the city, and the kids the parents were holding were actually local orphans. "I want another child," a woman quickly shouted, and an elderly man stepped forward and asked how he and his wife could be hired as foster parents as well. Before I knew it, over a dozen families in the crowd asked how they could apply for the program, and our foster network there quickly grew to include homes for over 30 children. For stay-at-home women who had raised their only child to adulthood, foster care was a beautiful second chance for them to be a mom again.

One of my favorite memories of visiting foster homes was when I climbed up six flights of stairs to a small apartment in the city of Kaifeng in Henan Province. I was met at the door by a cheerful woman in her 50s whose only child had already grown up and left the nest. In her arms was a two-year-old boy we had given the Western name of Luke. His eyes crinkled with a smile, and I gave silent thanks that we had found this wonderful mom for the little boy in front of me who had been born with Down Syndrome. I knew this was a special need which few families in China would readily accept, and so I gladly took a seat when the mom told me she wanted to tell me all about Luke and his accomplishments. She was well prepared for my visit, quickly putting a Chinese cap on his head and instructing him to welcome me to the home. Luke pressed his hands together in front of him and solemnly bowed, before breaking into a huge grin again as he checked with his mom to make sure he had done it properly. I then listened with joy as she made him imitate just about every animal noise I could think of, including moos, barks, and neighs. She kept pointing her finger to the top of his head, while saying, "Congming, congming" (so smart, so smart). I actually began to get a bit nervous, wondering if perhaps she didn't know that Luke was rocking an extra chromosome and thinking that she may change her mind about caring for him if she knew his special need. I turned to our foster care manager and whispered, "Does she know he has Down Syndrome?" Without missing a beat, our manager turned to the mom and posed that very question. "Oh yes, yes, yes," she replied quickly. And then she pointed to his head once again and said, "Congming, congming," with the smile of a very proud mom.

Luke absolutely bloomed in foster care, and I compared his progress many times with the children I knew in institutions who had been born with Down Syndrome. I would often see kids with this special need simply lying in cribs all day, with muscles so weak they could barely sit on their own. Luke met almost all of his developmental goals in record time, and when he turned four, his mom contacted our manager and said it was time for him to go to school just like other kids his age. Our manager called me and said, "I think we have a problem as no kindergarten will accept a child with Down Syndrome into their class." At first, we tried to explain to his mom that it just wouldn't be possible. But as I should have known, you should never get in front of a mama bear trying to protect her cub, and this foster mom was insistent that Luke deserved to go to school just like everyone else in their neighborhood. Negotiations with the local school began to try and convince them that inclusion would be a very wonderful thing. I sure wish I could have been a fly on the wall when Luke's foster mom took on that principal for the final time because the next day I got an email that he was officially enrolled – most definitely the first child with Down Syndrome to be included in public school in his town. Every morning, Luke's mom would walk him to school, firmly holding his hand with a satisfied smile on her face that she was doing everything in her power to give him the best life possible. I got to visit Luke at kindergarten one day, and, as I stood watching the other kids include him in their playground games, I gave thanks once again for the blessings of foster care. Little

Luke was firmly accepted as a treasured part of his community versus being confined to institutional care. He had shown me yet again that every child does indeed count and oh the strides they can make when they have their very own mom and dad as their champions.

Eleven

Cleft Trip – M*A*S*H Style

In 2005, after the success of our cleft trip the year before, we decided that we would send not one but TWO back-to-back surgical teams to China to heal children born with cleft lip. In a move that I would like to attribute to temporary insanity, I agreed that holding this new cleft trip inside an orphanage would be a wonderful idea, and we soon had a signed agreement to perform surgeries inside the Luoyang orphanage for a two-week period that fall. If you remember from an earlier chapter, just the year before I had asked myself, "How hard could it be to set up a cleft trip?" (Yes, I am obviously a slow learner.) I now found myself asking, "How hard could it be to set up a complete mobile operating room and recovery ward?" I believe the people working with me at that time were beginning to get just a wee bit nervous when I started posing questions like that.

It is important for me to mention that we do things a lot more differently now. We no longer hold "cleft missions" but instead organize "cleft exchanges," which are partnerships with Chinese hospitals where surgeons from the U.S. and China can share ideas and best practices. We now take the smallest number of people possible on these trips, since we don't want to disrupt the daily work of a hospital and want to work side by side with Chinese doctors and nurses as a team. But back in 2005, when we decided to set up our own mini hospital inside an orphanage in impoverished Henan Province, we headed to China with EIGHTY (yes, 80!) people ready to give their time to help kids in need. I look back on that trip and know that God was firmly in control as there is no other way to explain the success of that trip despite all the obstacles we faced upon arrival.

In what at the time we thought was an incredible stroke of good luck, we had been offered medical supplies and an OR table and lights from a different organization working in China. Each time I would send a list of things the medical team needed (sutures, scalpels, IV poles, oxygen meters), I would get an email back from the other group saying it was all covered. No worries at all….everything's under control. When we arrived at the orphanage that first day, however, to inventory what they had sent, we found boxes and boxes of expired medical supplies, outdated medications, and broken equipment. The enormous cardboard boxes were crushed and moldy, and, instead of setting up the OR that first afternoon, we instead found ourselves doing junk removal, carrying box after box outside to be burned. A frantic effort began to find everything we would need in the local markets instead. The good thing about having such a large team is that everyone could spread out and find what was needed, and I'm happy to report that by the next morning we had a fully stocked OR. New cots stretched as far as you could see in the enormous orphanage activity room, and our volunteers put up welcome signs and strung rope across the ceiling to hang mobile IV bags. It was really amazing to watch it all come together with everyone working as a united team.

Few people know even to this day that I had been given a list of over 120 children who needed cleft surgery by the same group who had sent the useless medical supplies, and so I probably should have been better prepared that next morning when I heard from their director that none of the children would be coming to see our team. None, as in ZERO. I was standing there holding a list in my hands of child after child who supposedly needed our help, complete with their names, birthdays, orphanages, and I think I went into a fugue state for a moment as I struggled to understand what I was being told. Was the man on the phone really saying that we had NO patients to heal? That none of the kids he had promised needed surgery were going to make it to our team? We had 80 volunteers who had flown all the way across the world to give their time! It was impossible to even comprehend as I was gripping that six-page patient list in my hand! Yes, that was a bad morning.

My co-leader on that trip was a wonderful person named Karen Maunu. She and I had never met in person before but had, of course, talked extensively by phone as all the trip arrangements were made. I liked her immediately upon meeting her at the airport, and the two of us quickly went into crisis mode as we started firing off ideas on how to salvage the trip. Henan was the most populous province in China at the time and had so many people living in complete poverty. Surely there were 100 children who could benefit from our team – but the question was how to find them. We decided it was time to bring in the media. If we could get the word out to orphanages and rural families that free medical help was available, surely some people would come forward, right?

Surgeries were supposed to begin the very next morning; so that afternoon Karen and I did newspaper and TV interview after interview. We knew we at least had a full surgery day for the first day as we had 16 kids on the list from the orphanage hosting us, but we had no idea how many more could be found. We were very soon to find out how many times a cell phone can ring in one day. If you guessed thousands and thousands, you would have guessed right. At least that is how it seemed after our phone number was published in the paper and shown on TV. We learned that the circulation of the newspapers we were in was approximately 11 million people. Yes, 11 with that many zeroes after it. Every time our Chinese director would hang up from one call, another would immediately come in. Whenever she got busy doing something else, when she returned to her phone it would say "Missed Calls: 45" or "Missed Calls: 92." When people couldn't reach her on the cell, they began text messaging, and they would explain in detail why their child needed to be seen by our team. The word overwhelming doesn't begin to describe it. It would have been impossible for our team to see even a fraction of the children whose parents and caregivers called. I began praying for a way to heal as many of them as possible.

The next morning, as I walked towards the orphanage gates, I saw a line of people stretching as far as I could see. Everywhere you looked there were families holding babies with cleft needs. Soon after, a huge, full-sized motor coach pulled up with babies from an orphanage in the neighboring province. The Datong orphanage had heard we were providing free surgeries, and they had come with 23 children in hand. We learned that news of our team had spread even as far as Inner Mongolia. As the week wore on, I would see families arriving who had walked for two to three days to reach our team – families who arrived with only the clothes on their backs but all with the hope that their children would finally get the cleft surgery they needed. It was very emotional for our team to realize that even working 24/7, we could never heal them all.

We decided that in order to reduce the number of people who were amassing outside the orphanage, we would talk to the waiting parents about the safety guidelines in place for the surgeries. We explained about the 10/10/10 rule and told the families that babies had to weigh at least ten pounds to qualify for general anesthesia. One of the nurses pulled me over to the side the next day and told me that the frantic parents who knew their babies weren't heavy enough had started sewing rocks into their children's clothing in order for them to qualify. We had also decided that no child over eight would receive palate surgery, in order to decrease some of the waiting crowd. The surgeons had explained to me that most kids' speech patterns with an open palate were pretty set by that age and that the surgery wouldn't be a huge benefit to them, versus a younger child whose speech could be more easily improved. I will never forget the panic in one rural father's eyes when we told him his ten-year-old son would not be receiving palate surgery. He walked away with tears in his eyes, firmly holding his son's hand. The next day I saw the father again. He pretended not to see me and determinedly came up to the registration table. I noticed he had shaved his son's head and they both had on new shirts, even though I know they had almost no money at all. I watched as he and his son sat down in the intake area to be interviewed by one of the nurses, pretending to be there for the first time. She asked him, "How old is your son?" Without missing a beat he firmly said, "He is seven." I didn't say a word and gave a silent prayer of thanks for a father's great love when I saw that the little boy was added to our surgery schedule.

As each day's OR list was created, parents waiting to hear whether their children were chosen for surgery would gather on the rooftop of the orphanage. I loved sitting with them and hearing their stories. It was on this trip that everything I thought I knew about birth parents in China was turned on its head. Up until that point, whenever I thought of my own daughter's story, I had a clear vision of her birth parents making that fateful decision to leave her. For some reason in my head, I always imagined it was the birth mother who made the decision, but I soon realized that the very real issue of child abandonment is a whole lot more complicated than that. Again and again, I talked to families who described the great difficulties they faced in keeping a child who was not wanted by the extended family. Many of the parents shared very openly with us that they had to hide their child with cleft from their relatives, knowing they would never be accepted in Chinese society. They told us they would bring great shame to their family if they refused to abandon their children, and many of the parents began crying when telling us how much they loved their kids. We met a father who brought his son to see our team, and he told us that he had hidden the child for six whole years, afraid that his family would insist that the little boy be given away. His son was now of school age, however, and he would soon need to be out in public if he was to ever have an education. The dad said, "I am praying you will accept him as a patient, so my son can have some hope for a happy future. I cannot think of being parted from him."

Another couple who came to our trip arrived on what I believe was complete fate. One of our Chinese directors, who was coming to Henan Province by train, saw the young couple holding a baby while the mother cried and cried. He finally asked them what was wrong and learned that the couple was from a province far to the west. They had been told by their parents that their little boy, born with cleft, was not welcome in the family since he would bring a curse to them. Too heartbroken and ashamed to leave their beloved baby in their own province, this couple boarded a train to abandon the son that they loved with all their hearts. I still consider it divine fortune that our director met them on that train heading east. I got a phone call from him asking if he could bring the couple with him to see our team and of course told him to get there as quickly as he could. It is still amazing to me that we were able to provide surgery to this little boy, as they had left their home province with the mandate by their family to abandon him. Instead, they traveled home a few weeks later, with their cherished son having a brand-new smile.

All of our team's hearts were touched when a peasant farmer arrived in Luoyang with his six-year-old daughter who had an extremely complex bilateral cleft lip. The father told us that he had found the little girl in a field when she was a baby, and his heart was so moved by her cries that had taken her in to be her father. He told us that when he had decided to send her to school this year, she was beaten by bullies for looking so different. Again moved by compassion, he had decided to simply keep her home, to safely work with him in the fields, although he still dreamed that someday she could have an education. He asked us if it would be possible for her to have surgery that very day. When it was explained that the surgery schedule for Friday was already full and that no surgeries would take place on Saturday as the surgical teams switched, the father became very sad. He explained that he had to leave his crops in order to come see our team, and there was no way the tender plants would survive any longer without him.

We promised this man that his daughter could be first up for surgery on Sunday, and we asked for his phone number so that we could contact him, but he explained that he had never used a telephone before. He told us yet again that he couldn't stay in Luoyang until Sunday because his fields needed to be worked. We offered to keep the little girl with us on her own so he could return back home, and he turned and asked his little girl if that would be okay. When she heard the tentative plan, the little girl began crying, saying, "Daddy, please don't leave me." He knelt down and assured her that she was the most important thing in his life, and he told us he would be staying by her side. What a beautiful sacrifice from an adoptive father for his daughter.

Time and again, I saw these stories of hope and realized how little I knew about what it really means to live day-to-day in extreme poverty. We are almost all so guilty of taking what we have for granted. For instance, how many pictures do most of us have of those we hold dear, or how many times do we snap a photo on our cell phone and delete it when it isn't quite perfect? We realized on this trip that the majority of the families coming to see us were so poor that they didn't even have a single photograph of their child. One mom saw us taking a post-op photo of her little girl and nervously asked if she could please have one, too. We quickly printed out a copy for her. Later that night, I saw her staring intently at her daughter's image and rubbing her thumb over the photo of the child she loved so much. The only picture she had of her daughter was taken just hours post-surgery; so the little girl's face was bloody and swollen. Yet the simple piece of paper with her daughter's image was clearly a real treasure to her.

The next morning, an 11-year old girl with unrepaired cleft lip walked in off the street and bravely asked us if she could be healed. Her family worked as rural rice farmers and lived on less than $1 per day, and she told us they could never save enough to have her surgery be done in a hospital. When our team told her that she could definitely have the operation she needed, she began to cry. Between sobs, she told us she couldn't believe that she finally might be accepted in her village. We told the girl and her dad to please go back to their home, and we would call them with a definite surgery date later in the week; but they also told us they had never used a phone before. The little girl's mom had stayed behind in their village to work the fields while she sent her husband and daughter off on the long journey to Luoyang. They had no way to contact her to let her know they were safe. It brought tears to my eyes to think of the impoverished mother waiting back at home and wondering, "Will the strangers on the medical team choose her? Can my daughter finally get the help she needs?" I wish I could have seen the moment when the father and daughter walked up the dirt path to the family home to show the anxious mom that surgery had indeed taken place.

I had first begun working in China to help those who lived in orphanages, but the cleft trip in 2005 broke open my heart to all of the children and families living in such complete poverty. Repeatedly on that trip, I saw the deep love that these families had for their children born with medical needs. Their desperation to make their children's lives better humbled me, and their anguish in wanting their children to be accepted was so clear. Repeatedly, I was told that it was relatives who said that the child could not stay within the family circle. I met mothers who told me of falling asleep after delivery only to wake up in the morning and discover that their in-laws had taken a baby deemed "less than perfect" to abandon.

There is one mother, however, who still haunts me to this day. Because of the large crowds outside the orphanage, I had told our staff not to let anyone come inside to be evaluated who was less than four months of age. I was working near the OR when I saw a woman, obviously in distress, come through the doors holding a tiny bundle in her arms, clearly a newborn. Already overwhelmed by the number of families we had been forced to turn away, I told our Chinese director to let the woman know that we unfortunately wouldn't be able to see her child. I watched her walk over to the woman and then saw the young mom fall on her knees. After a few moments of conversation, our director came over and told me that I needed to speak with the woman in private. The three of us went into a back room, and the mother began to tell me her story.

In China, it is very common for women in the rural countryside to have a period of confinement for 30 days after delivery. They do not leave the house during this time, and they must avoid eating certain foods or doing certain activities so that good energy can surround both the mother and child. The mom explained that she was on the 28th day of her confinement, and she had snuck out of the house without anyone knowing after hearing about our team. As she began sobbing, she kept saying, "Please heal my daughter. I love her, I love her." She pulled back the blanket to show a beautiful little girl born with a simple unilateral cleft lip. She explained to me that her in-laws had said that the child could not stay in their home as the baby would bring bad luck and shame to the family circle. She explained that in three days, when her period of confinement was up, they were coming to take the little girl away from her. This young woman grabbed my hand, looked me right in the eyes and said, "Please help me. Please help me keep my baby." It broke my heart to know that there was absolutely nothing I could do surgically for her at that moment in time, as it wasn't safe to put her baby under general anesthesia inside an orphanage at 28 days of age. Perhaps if we were in a modern hospital, with the best monitoring equipment and anesthesia machines, the doctors could have tried, but the reality is that we were working in a mobile OR, and so it just wasn't possible.

I explained to her that the initial surgery for her child would not be a complex one, and that there were wonderful hospitals in China that could do the surgery. I told her that her daughter needed to weigh ten pounds and be three to four months of age before she could safely have the surgery she needed. Her eyes filled with tears once more, and I gripped her hands tightly, telling her that she needed to go somewhere and hide. She needed to go somewhere with her baby and hide until her child reached the weight where she could safely have the operation. I went and got my purse, and I took out $500 and pressed it into her hands, telling her that it would be enough for her child to receive cleft surgery at a Chinese hospital. I kept asking her, "Do you understand? Take your daughter and go someplace safe so that you can stay together."

We stood there together crying and holding hands while she nodded her head yes. She left the hospital that day with her back straight, clutching her tiny baby daughter with tears still streaming down her face. I was shaken to the core, and I will never know what happened to that baby girl. Did her grandparents come a few days later and wrench her from her mother's arms to abandon her? Did her mom find the strength to find a place to hide until her daughter was four months old and could receive surgery? I will never know, but I think of her often, especially as I look at my own kids from China.

What I learned on this life-changing trip is that far too often those of us who are adoptive parents like simple rose-colored answers to our children's beginnings. We like to find comfort in saying that the birth mother made a plan for our child or made an unselfish decision to give up the baby for a better life. Newspaper articles on child abandonment often cover the issue in blanket terms: "Babies are abandoned because rural families want sons." "Babies are abandoned because their medical needs are too great." Simple one-line sentences to explain a personal life event that is often very complex. Over and over on this trip, I heard individual stories from birth parents on why they were told their children could not stay in the extended family, and every story was unique. I met a woman whose daughter with cleft had been taken from her by her in-laws while she slept. She never saw her daughter again. She had come to see our team after reading about it in the paper to thank us for giving parents a chance to keep their children, a chance she herself did not have.

When it comes to human life and heartbreaking decisions – such as abandonment and loss – I have learned that there are rarely simple explanations. Every single child who has been adopted from China faced a great loss in their lives, but the reality is we rarely have any idea about the deep, personal stories of the people involved. We have no idea who made the decision that a child couldn't stay in the family. We have no idea of the anguish, or sacrifice, or resignation experienced. It is easy to think it was a birth parent who lovingly placed the child by the orphanage front gate, but it could have just as easily been an in-law, an uncle, or a friend who was given instructions by the head of the family to remove the baby from the home.

We can never forget that every child has his or her own unique story. Yes, some birth parents definitely do make plans. Other children are orphaned when their parents pass away. But we also have to acknowledge those birth parents who had their children taken from them or who felt pressured to give a child away so as not to bring shame to the family name. Anything we can do to help these desperate families have other choices is a blessing we cannot measure. I have never been in their shoes, and I know only a fraction of what they live through each day, but their stories have touched me to the center of my heart.

Twelve

Hercules

Have you ever had a mentor? Someone you could really look up to and who would honestly tell you when you were doing things right and wrong? I think everybody needs one, especially when just starting a new experience and journeying into the unknown. At the very beginning of our work in China, God blessed me immensely by putting two remarkable people in my life. When LWB first started, I had this pretty naïve thought that all charities would basically stand on a hillside together singing the classic Coca-Cola song about filling the world with love. We were all on the same side of "doing good," right? While I hate to burst anyone's bubble who has the same thought I had, the reality is that the charity world can be an extremely competitive place, and not everyone "plays well with others." This was really a difficult lesson for me to accept, but thankfully on one of my initial trips to Beijing I was introduced to Joyce and Robin Hill, the founders of New Hope. Joyce was a family practice physician from Australia, and her husband Robin was a very successful businessman from the U.K. They had moved to China in 1994, and, after a visit to a local orphanage, God placed the call to care for the orphaned firmly on both of their hearts. They began taking in abandoned children, and eventually, as the number of babies who needed them increased, they built the Hope Foster Home on a very peaceful parcel of land outside of Beijing. The first time I walked through the doors of this home, I knew something absolutely beautiful was taking place there.

I will never forget the first dinner I had with the Hills. We sat together in their kitchen while Robin made a stir fry, and I had a thousand questions to ask about how they were successfully working in China. I will always remember that they spent hours that first evening sharing some of the lessons they had learned with me. When I left that night, Robin said I could call him at any time with additional questions. They didn't look at what we were trying to do with LWB as competition. Instead, they hugged me and said, "There can never be enough of us working together to help the orphaned." It was the start of a beautiful and remarkable friendship that I still treasure to this day. Their wisdom and compassion have helped us many times, and the children we have healed together are too numerous to count. There is one little boy, however, whose life always makes me think of this very special couple. Baby Hercules, as he came to be known, taught me so much about just how hard a tiny baby can fight each day.

Hercules was born with cleft lip and palate, and, when he came into the world, he was already too tiny to survive being abandoned. But somehow he did. When the police found him and brought him to the orphanage in his town, he weighed less than four pounds. You couldn't really call him a beautiful baby, but immediately the orphanage knew he was a determined baby. Even as a newborn, they told me he would lie awake in his crib looking around. His orphanage was a very poor one, down a long rural road, and, even though the women who were caring for him were kind-hearted, they were also extremely busy trying to make sure all the babies in their care got at least a few bottles each day. Hercules, however, struggled to feed from the moment he entered orphanage care. When he tried to take a bottle, he would choke and gasp. He wanted to eat (boy, did he want to eat!), but it just didn't work for him because of his cleft lip and wide palate. As the months went by, he didn't seem to grow any bigger in size. In fact, by the time two adoptive families visiting his orphanage saw him for the first time, he was alarmingly malnourished; so much so that the families frantically called their adoption agency in tears, who then called us to see if there was any way we could help.

Thankfully, our cleft trip in Luoyang was going on that very week, and so we called the orphanage director to see if there was any possibility they could bring the baby to see our medical team, even though we were on the whole other side of the province with many rural roads between us. The director at that time was a truly kind man and was so happy that someone might be able to help this failure-to-thrive baby that they were in a car on their way to see us within 30 minutes of that first phone call. Six hours later they arrived, and I will never forget them hurrying into the room to bring baby Hercules to us. They had little Hercules all bundled up in blankets, but immediately I could see that he was far too tiny for his age. Yet there was something so amazing about his eyes. They were the eyes of an "old soul," looking far too wise in his wrinkled face. He stared at me intently, and once again I found myself holding a baby who was silently pleading for help with his gaze.

Our whole team fell in love with this tiny little boy. Our volunteers gave him a warm bath, and we wrapped him up in new clothes and a blanket. Then we got out the cleft bottle. For those of you who are unfamiliar with them, cleft bottles are "squeezie" bottles, which are soft-bodied versus the standard hard plastic. Caregivers are able to squeeze the formula into the baby's mouth, rather than making them suck on their own, which they often can't do. Back then, cleft bottles couldn't be bought in China, but they were absolutely essential to tiny babies who struggled to feed. We filled up one of these special bottles with warm formula, and Hercules had the first full meal of his life. I don't think any of us had a dry eye when he finished.

For the next 24 hours, our volunteers rocked and held him but most of all fed him. One volunteer curled up on a cot and placed baby Hercules right next to her to sleep. He was all bundled up and warmed by the heat of her body, and I am sure he had some of his sweetest dreams ever that night.

By the next day, he was already looking better, with much more alert eyes, but he was nowhere near heavy enough to have a cleft operation, weighing in at just seven pounds at five months of age. When we broke the news to the orphanage staff that we couldn't yet do his surgery, they were visibly disappointed. They had been so hopeful he could be healed. After a few days of staying with our team, we sent the nannies home with a bag full of cleft bottles and several huge cans of the best formula we could find. We assured them that as soon as this little boy hit ten pounds, we would make sure he had surgery. All of us hated to see him go. We had loved holding him, and, I think since he was the size of a newborn, we had really enjoyed sitting on a cot rocking him and singing soft lullabies. Boy, did he have a tight grip! He constantly reached for the hand of the person holding him, and he would grab onto their finger and refuse to let go. When we finally had to say goodbye, I admit that I started to cry, wondering if he could keep that fighting spirit inside of him. Every day after I got back home to Oklahoma, I would pray for baby Hercules.

In late December, a few months after returning from China, I got a feeling in my heart so strong that I had to go to his orphanage. It felt like a quick intake of breath, and I heard the words so clearly: "Go to Henan." But that was crazy of course because I had just gotten back from China, and we didn't have any ongoing programs in that province yet. I kept trying to rationally shake off the feeling that I had to return, but the message in my heart was firm and strong. I needed to get on a plane to China as quickly as arrangements could be made.

As I walked into Hercules' rural orphanage for the first time in January, there was only one baby on my mind, and he was in the second crib over. There was little Hercules, sucking on his two fingers the same way he had on the cleft trip, and looking just as wise as ever. He was still incredibly tiny, and, as I held him, I knew in my heart that he was at the very end of his battle. He somehow seemed even smaller than when I had seen him a few months before, and his arms and legs had redundant skin that just hung from his bones. His nannies told us how much they wanted him to gain weight after the cleft trip, but they kept saying there were simply not enough hands. "He needs one-on-one care," they told me. Even as they said it, I knew exactly where he needed to be. This little boy needed to go to Beijing, to the Hope Foster Home, where he could have his own aunty who was trained to work with little fighters like him.

I knew that the Hills often had a long waiting list of babies needing medical care. With a deep breath, I borrowed my friend's cell phone and rang Dr. Joyce. "There is this baby...," I began as always. "How fast can you get him here?" she answered right back.

As I hung up the phone, I knew that Hercules was going to make it. I also knew that he was indeed the reason I was standing in China at that very moment. Would you fly all the way across the world to help just one child? I think most of us would. As huge, white snowflakes began to fall outside the door of the orphanage, my friend Karen and I each took one more turn holding this precious baby. As I kissed his forehead, I whispered to him that I knew he was destined for great things.

The next day, we began our trip to the airport, which became one of the most treacherous journeys I have ever experienced. At the time, we didn't know we were in the middle of one of the worst blizzards to ever hit the region. Our van actually had two near misses of what could have easily been fatal accidents. During one of them, we did several complete 360 turns on the highway ice before ending up precariously on the edge of a steep hill. It was one of those surreal moments where time slowed down and I could see the huge bus we were going to collide with... but somehow didn't. As we all sat stunned in our seats with our hearts pounding, our local van driver suddenly shouted out, "My mom is a Christian!", which broke the terrified silence and had us all laughing together. For the rest of the dangerous journey, however, I noticed that despite our nervous smiles to each other, all of our hands continued to shake as we each silently prayed for protection.

We finally reached the airport many hours later, and the orphanage director and I both got down on our knees to literally kiss the frozen ground that we had arrived safely. Karen and I headed inside with the blowing snow swirling around us and, of course, quickly learned that all flights in and out of the province were canceled. We sat in the Zhengzhou airport for almost two days, with a violent blizzard raging outside. People around us were understandably angry and upset, but Karen and I couldn't stop smiling. We both had a peace in our hearts that I cannot even describe. It didn't matter that we were snowed in, and it didn't matter that we couldn't feel our toes any more since they had shut off all the power and heat inside the terminal. All that mattered is that we had come to China to see one tiny little boy, who would soon be on his way to healing. We just kept smiling and hugging each other in joy. We must have been so out of place among all of the anger and frustration because more than one group of people came up to us to say, "Why are you having fun? Let us in on your secret." Laughing to each other, we would reply, "We are just SO HAPPY!"

Because of the blizzard in the region, getting little Hercules to Beijing was going to be difficult. But the orphanage said that they would move him as soon as they could. All of the trains were sold out for the upcoming Chinese Spring Festival, the biggest holiday of the year, when millions of Chinese people travel home. Finally, they were able to find two tickets to Beijing on a train leaving New Year's Day. In China, Spring Festival is a time typically spent with one's family, just like our Christmas, and no one wants to work on a holiday. I think it speaks volumes that his nannies wanted to help him so much that they said without a second thought, "We'll take those tickets." And so on New Year's Day, two caregivers and baby Hercules boarded a train to his new life at Hope Foster Home. He began downing a full cleft bottle every three hours and charmed everyone with his wise little eyes. Dr. Hill shared with me that upon arrival to their home, he was in the beginning stages of organ failure. Without intervention, he would have lived just a few more days.

When I think of Hercules, I think of the many children I have known who have beaten the odds. I look at his early photos, and I say a prayer of thanksgiving that he is still part of this world. One of my dear friends told me that it is impossible to fully measure the worth of one person's life because that person will go on to touch others, who will touch others... in a never-ending cycle of humanity. That is why our work is so important, and that is why we can never grow weary of trying to help those who need us most.

Several years ago, I was honored to see Hercules once again, this time with his adoptive family and looking the very picture of strength and health. As he shyly gave me a hug, I couldn't help but wonder about the lasting footsteps he is leaving on this earth. Maybe he'll grow up to be a doctor, or an incredible teacher, or maybe he will be a loving daddy someday. That's the exciting part about any of us having a future though, isn't it? Realizing that so many unknown chapters have yet to be written. For Hercules, even though he is just a boy, his story is already a remarkable one. I am confident that the best is still to come.

Thirteen

Gong Lu

Over the years, we have been blessed to partner with physicians from all over the world in order to provide the very best medical care to the kids who come into our hands. These are amazing doctors, many who have advanced their fields, and yet they are never too busy to take a call from us about an orphaned child who needs help.

One of the physicians who volunteered with LWB several times was Dr. Lisa Buckmiller, a pediatric ENT doctor who also specializes in vascular facial surgery. At the time, she was based out of Arkansas Children's Hospital, doing extensive humanitarian work around the world. We were thrilled when she agreed to come on an LWB cleft trip, and I really enjoyed getting to know her more in China. During our initial talks together, I, of course, asked about her family. She explained that she and her husband Richard had decided not to have children because her work and travel schedule to help kids in need kept her far too busy. This wasn't the decision her mother wanted to hear as she wanted to be a grandma so badly, but Lisa said they had made up their minds to remain childless. There were actually several nurses and physicians on that trip who didn't have children at the time. Those of us who were adoptive parents were honestly quite merciless in our campaign that week to convince them that adoption is a wonderful way to grow a family. Many of the kids having surgery with us that week were actually already on adoption agency lists, just waiting to be chosen, and so we would take every opportunity to plop one of those beautiful babies into their laps, saying "Can you hold him for just a second while we run an errand?" Oh yes, we were relentless, and I'm happy to say that several adoptions did indeed come from that trip. But Dr. Buckmiller shook her head at me and just said, "Nice try."

Shortly after returning to the U.S., we were contacted by a woman who had recently gone to an orphanage in central China to adopt her newest daughter. While there, she had been greeted by a little girl named Gong Lu, who seemed to be the official welcoming committee for the orphanage. To say that Gong Lu had personality galore is a massive understatement as she absolutely radiated joy and vivacity. It was clear from the families we talked to that this was a very special five-year-old, who would grab your hand the moment you walked through the door, but whose paperwork wasn't submitted for adoption herself because of an enormous facial tumor originating from her nose. Gong Lu had watched baby after baby leave the orphanage with new families, sadly wondering if it would ever be her turn. It is so painful to think about what all the older children in orphanages must feel when they are told by caregivers that they will never be chosen themselves.

The mom who contacted us could not get this little girl out of her mind. She sent us a photo of Gong Lu by email, and we immediately knew that the tumor would define her entire life in China if she didn't get medical care. It took up almost a third of her face, and I was sure that it must have been very hard on Gong Lu's heart to continually hear negative comments about the way she looked. Local doctors feared that trying to operate on Gong Lu could actually endanger her life as the large tumor was such a complex maze of blood vessels that there could be massive blood loss during surgery. At the same time that the adoptive mom called LWB, she also contacted Dr. Buckmiller as she was such a well-known specialist in this very type of tumor. We all immediately agreed that we would work together to make sure Gong Lu finally got the medical care she needed.

We started by making arrangements for Gong Lu to travel to Beijing for an MRI in order to get a clearer picture on whether the tumor was even operable. Thankfully, it was. Then the decision was made that, due to its enormous size, it would be preferable to bring Gong Lu to the United States for surgery, so that Dr. Buckmiller could operate with her own team and equipment. The MRI showed that the tumor was highly vascular, and the number of blood vessels involved meant the surgery would be extremely complex.

Within just a matter of weeks, everything started falling into place for Gong Lu to come to America. She received her passport and temporary medical visa, and Arkansas Children's generously agreed to waive all the fees for her treatment – an absolutely amazing gift. Arrangements were made for Gong Lu to travel with her orphanage director, Ms. Xu, a soft-spoken and kind woman beloved by the parents who had adopted children from her facility. She cared deeply about the kids in her orphanage, even writing personal letters each year to those who were adopted overseas asking them to stay in touch. She shared with us that Gong Lu was known as "Red Nose" in China, and that the little girl had been wishing her entire life to look normal. Excitement began to build in the orphanage as more people learned that this tiny ray of sunshine was finally getting her chance to be healed. Before leaving to travel to the U.S., local officials threw her a party and hung a huge banner in the orphanage courtyard wishing her well on her journey. Gong Lu told everyone, "After the surgery, I hope to be a beautiful girl. Then I would like to go to school like other children."

Ms. Xu was understandably nervous about the trip as neither she nor Gong Lu had ever flown on an airplane before. Since the operation was going to be in Little Rock, they would have to go through immigration and transfer planes at the very busy Chicago O'Hare airport. Don't ever let anyone convince you that our world is going completely downhill because the reality is that it is still filled with such kind and giving people. Every step of their journey was filled with small acts of love, from the employees at a software company who pooled their frequent flyer miles and money to purchase their international air tickets, to the airport staff in Chicago who made sure a Mandarin speaker was there as they got off the plane to help them through customs. When they finally landed late at night in Little Rock, they were met by a crowd of people with welcome signs. Gong Lu was so excited to be handed a bouquet of brightly colored balloons, and she held on to them tightly as they waited for their luggage. When it was time to get into the car, she handed them back to the man who had presented them to her while sweetly saying, "Thank you for letting me play with them!" Kids in orphanages rarely have anything that is completely "theirs," and she hadn't realized it was a gift just for her.

Up until this point, I had only known Gong Lu through her photos and the stories that adoptive parents had shared with me about her joyful personality; so I was really excited to drive over to Little Rock to be with her during the surgery. I wrote to the LWB volunteers afterwards that I had tried my best to come up with the exact right words to describe her spirit, but then I decided it would be like trying to describe a sunset with a single sentence or trying to describe standing on the shore of an ocean for the first time. You would have had to be there to fully understand the depth of it, and so nothing I could ever write would do justice to this little girl who captured my heart so deeply.

As I pulled up to the home in Little Rock where she was staying, she ran up and gave me a hug, calling me "Ayi Amy." I quickly learned that despite never having ridden a bike in China, she had mastered it perfectly within minutes of trying. She could shoot a basketball like a pro (she was 3 for 3 when she was playing against me), and every new experience she was having outside the orphanage walls brought an absolute burst of giggles. We had brought her some very small presents, and one of them was a bubble necklace that she immediately wanted to try. When the first bubbles magically formed in the air, she clapped her hands with glee, and her smile lit up her entire face. Her intelligence astounded me as she was already picking up English words, and she would just chat away excitedly in Chinese, telling us how happy she was to be getting this opportunity. She announced to everyone that her dreams for the future included getting "this thing" off her nose, finding a family, growing up, getting married, and definitely becoming a doctor who could heal other kids. I learned all of that within the first 15 minutes of my visit with her! She had been given a pretend doctor's kit, which she took out to show me with excitement. She insisted I lay down on the floor and then she took my blood pressure, checked my heart, and even gave me a shot. After each check, she would say "hao de, hao de," (good, good), like she was very impressed with the results.

Next, it was time for a rousing game of hide-and-seek, made all the more fun by the language barrier and the fact that Gong Lu chose the same place to hide each time, giggling so loudly that she quickly gave away her location. At one point in the afternoon, she accidentally closed her hand completely in a closet door, and she tried very hard to be brave while a dark blister began forming on her little finger. Without thinking, I kissed her pinky, and she gave me a look like she had never seen that done before. She must have decided that it helped some though as for the rest of the night, every time I saw her she presented her pinky to me for a "get well" kiss.

The funniest part of the day was when we took a walk on the beautiful golf course behind the home of the family who was hosting Gong Lu during her time in the U.S. It was evening, and so I didn't think anyone would be out golfing at that time. We walked down to a cool stream, and she learned how to throw stones in the water. We were coming back on the fairway when someone suddenly yelled, "FORE!" The ball came flying out of nowhere right in front of us, and suddenly I saw Gong Lu dart onto the fairway to grab it. She took off running down the course with the golfer yelling, "Stop! Stop!" I was laughing so hard as I chased after her. She did NOT want to give up that nice little white ball that someone had so conveniently hit her way, but she definitely improved the golfer's lie when she finally agreed to drop it as she had sprinted at least 50 yards closer to the hole.

The very next day was Gong Lu's big surgery, and everyone had to be at the hospital at 5:30 in the morning. She was so brave during all the blood draws, even though she had two big tears well up in her eyes. After her labs were finished, I walked over to the bed to rub her leg, and she must have recognized me as the "pinky lady," because she held up her arm where they had drawn the blood for me to kiss it. Isn't it amazing how well that works with kids?

Soon after, it was time for Gong Lu to head back to the operating suite. LWB's medical director and I were allowed to gown up and go into the OR as well to watch the entire surgery. Truly, it was nothing short of miraculous to watch Dr.

Buckmiller's concentration and skills as she painstakingly removed the tumor. It took almost two hours to fully release it, and then several more to sculpt and create a new nose for Gong Lu. Dr. Buckmiller is not only a wonderful person and doctor, but I realized that day that facial surgeons are also true artists, as we watched her meticulous methods to get Gong Lu's nose as close to perfect as possible. After over five hours in the OR, we gathered around a still sleeping Gong Lu. Many of us were crying at her beautiful new face, which now matched the beauty of her spirit. As I stood by the operating table and stared at her new nose, I was filled with such an incredible feeling of happiness and thanksgiving that this little girl had finally received the surgery she needed. I didn't know then that even greater things were already starting to take shape on the horizon.

Before Gong Lu's surgery, we had received a phone call from NBC's "Today Show" that they wanted to share her inspirational story. Camera crews from NBC had actually been documenting her care at Arkansas Children's Hospital, and they had spent time with Gong Lu and her foster family in Little Rock. During each interview, she would look straight into the camera and say that her biggest dream after the surgery was to find a "good mama and daddy who can adopt me." In fact, in the pre-surgery interview with Dr. Buckmiller as well, Lisa said that Gong Lu had made it clear she wanted to find a family. She hoped the operation would finally allow her to do just that.

NBC told us that they wanted to air Gong Lu's story about a month after the operation took place. They invited our medical director and Dr. Buckmiller to come to New York with Gong Lu for an in-person interview with Katie Couric and Matt Lauer. They rolled out the red carpet for this wonderful little girl, who excitedly got to visit the Statue of Liberty, Central Park, and, of course, Rockefeller Studios the morning of the show. Over the years, I had watched Katie Couric interview hundreds of guests and had seen many children sit across from her on the Today Show, but I had never seen what happened with Gong Lu that morning. Dressed in a new pink outfit and wearing a bow in her hair, she climbed up into Katie's lap and sat contentedly there the entire interview. When asked, "What do you think about the operation?" she replied in her sweet little voice, "I am now a beautiful girl. Thank you aunties, thank you doctors. I am so happy."

The next part of the interview came as a complete surprise, however. In front of the rolling cameras, Dr. Buckmiller made the announcement that she and her husband had started adoption paperwork in order to hopefully become Gong Lu's parents. Remember the doctor who had told me on our cleft trip that she had decided never to become a mother? I always loved that Yiddish proverb that if you want to make God laugh, just state your plans. In this case, He had listened to Lisa definitively state that motherhood wasn't in her cards and then smiled down on her with a pint-sized little girl from a Chinese orphanage. When Gong Lu heard the translation of what had just been said, she replied back on live TV that she definitely wanted Dr. Lisa as her mommy. I don't think there was a dry eye across America that morning. The little girl who had watched with longing as baby after baby was adopted without her finally had her dream of finding a "good mama and daddy" come true.

Fourteen

TJ Hao

There is one thing about getting involved in orphan care that everyone should know. Once you start meeting the children and learning their stories, your heart will never be the same again. And for many people in the adoption community, once you see the incredible transformations which occur when a child finally joins a forever family, you often find yourself looking at the waiting child lists wondering if you could possibly add just one more blessing to your home. I tell our volunteers all the time that while humanitarian aid to orphanages is critical and important and essential, nothing changes the life of an orphaned child the way adoption does. Four words I say again and again to my own kids and to anyone who will listen are these: WE ALL NEED FAMILY.

A few years after I first started working in China, I knew without a doubt that there was one more child who needed to join our home. Every time I would pray about it, I would tell God that I hoped He would let me know which little girl it was supposed to be. At the time, I had four boys and two girls, and so I just knew we needed another daughter to finalize our family.

Several months later, I was in China again and walked into an orphanage baby room, where I felt a pull on my heart to go to the back wall. I can't describe it exactly, but it was like I was being magnetically led to the back corner of the room, and I found myself standing over a little boy in a baby walker who had on a bright yellow sweater. His jet black hair stuck straight up all over his head, and he had red bug bites all over his face. He stuck out his tongue at me, and I immediately broke into a smile. We had done a lot of work for this orphanage over the years, and so I knew the nannies were always wanting to make sure my visits were good ones. One of them ran over and tried to steer me to some of the tinier babies in the room, but I reached down and picked up the little guy in front of me and settled him onto my hip. He looked like he was about two. As I ran my hands over his brillo pad hairdo, he leaned in for what I thought was going to be a kiss. I was just a wee bit startled when he bit me firmly on my cheek instead! To say the nanny in the room was panicked is an understatement. She rushed over and tried to take him out of my arms, but I assured her (even as I was feeling my cheek to see if there were actual teeth marks there) that perhaps that was just his own unique way of welcoming me. She quickly rolled up the arm of his knitted yellow sweater to show me that he was missing his right forearm and tried to get me to go over and hold a different baby instead, but by now little Hao (as I learned he was called) had settled his legs firmly around my waist and appeared to have claimed me as his own. I didn't know if it translated well, but I told the nanny that instead of love at first sight, I was sure this was love at first bite.

After I returned to the U.S., I began praying again about adoption, and I heard God so clearly speak to my heart that the little boy in yellow was supposed to be my final child. This did not fit with my carefully mapped out plan of my family, which I was certain was supposed to be four boys and THREE girls. I actually got on my knees and started having a little argument with God, telling Him that I really didn't think it was a BOY. I was sure that with all the little girls in orphanages also needing homes, certainly one of them was supposed to be Anna's little sister. This went on for several weeks, with me hearing clearly when I prayed that I was supposed to adopt the little boy in yellow while I would keep looking at waiting child lists for the daughter I knew I was going to have. Finally I told God that if Hao was really the child I was supposed to bring home, then he would basically have to drop into my lap as I would never use my connections with LWB to try and arrange his adoption. I didn't even know if his paperwork had been filed; so how could God be telling me to bring him home? Just three days later, I got an email from a woman volunteering with an adoption agency saying they had just gotten in a group of kids' files from an orphanage we worked with, and the very first name mentioned was little Hao. Yep, he had fallen directly into my lap. I sat quietly at my desk for a moment before picking up the phone and calling their China coordinator. I told her, "I think you need to pencil my name next to his file because I believe God is showing me we're supposed to bring that little guy home." She emailed me the photo in his adoption file, and darn if he wasn't wearing yet another yellow outfit, this one with a giant "E" on the front of it (as in "Eldridge"). Ten months later, TJ Hao became the seventh and final child in our family, and none of us could imagine our lives without him. Note to self: Quit trying to win arguments with God.

TJ had spent almost two more years in institutional care than my daughter Anna had, and it was a sobering thought to me that he had gone through his entire infancy without parents. I wondered how long it would take for him to learn his place in our home and how long it would be until he understood fully that we were now a permanent FAMILY. It ended up being a simple run to a Target store which hammered home to me just what that word can mean to a child's heart.

TJ absolutely loves animals, and he has ever since he was a baby. The nannies at his orphanage told me that once he could walk, he would push his wheeled metal crib over to the window so he could climb up and see a little dog that was sometimes tied in a neighboring yard. Through our education program in his orphanage, we had delivered lots of brightly colored books to the school there. I have several photos of TJ before his adoption looking at animal books, completely mesmerized at the beautiful images of tigers and bears in front of him.

Once he was adopted, he couldn't go into a zoo shop or toy store without wanting to stop and linger at the miniature plastic animals he would see on the shelves. I admit I was a complete sucker for his fascination, and so we began collecting toy animals for him to play with at home. One day, when we were out getting groceries, we walked over to the toy aisle so he could stop at the animal display. He kept trying to place two zebras into the shopping cart, and I kept insisting that we would only buy one. I took the second zebra from the cart and placed it back on the shelf, and TJ's eyes filled with tears. He actually cried all the way out of the store, trying desperately to tell me why he needed both zebras, but since he only had a few words in his vocabulary at that time, his pleas didn't work. I kept assuring him that he only needed one. "It's never good to be greedy, sweetheart," I told him. But he kept stretching out his arms pointing back towards the storefront, still hoping for the other.

Every time we would go into another shop with animals over the next few months, he would always try to buy two. Mom, being thrifty, would say, "We only need one panda," or "TJ, you should be happy with one cow." And he would always look so sadly at the toys as we walked away.

116

It wasn't until his English language finally began to grow that I finally understood the depth of TJ's desire to always have two animals. One day he was carefully searching through his bucket of toys until he found two lions. He put one up on the table first and said "baby," and then with great care he put up the second, right next to the first, and earnestly said, "MOM." He dug some more into his bucket and managed to find two elephants. He once again placed the first one on the table saying, "baby," and then gently sat the larger one down near the other while saying to himself with great relief, "MOM."

Oh yes, my heart fell to my toes. TJ had realized so profoundly after his adoption that babies need moms, and that was the source of his distress when I would only allow him to buy one animal at a time. He had been trying to tell me at the age of three that his baby zebra needed a mommy because it wasn't right for a child to be alone. How could I not have seen that? From that point forward, we always bought our animals in family groups because TJ was so concerned that every baby must have a parent to take care of them.

It is from seeing that longing in a child's heart so many times over the last decade that keeps me as a staunch advocate for international adoption even though I know there are many people firmly in the camp that a child should never leave their homeland. Every child on this earth has a basic human right to be raised in a family, however, regardless of country. Children are NOT supposed to be raised in institutions. As I have said a thousand times, it is not rocket science... kids need families. Nope. Strike that. We ALL need families.

Through my work, I have met hundreds of orphaned children who ended up aging out of the adoption process at age 14, without ever being chosen by a permanent mom or dad. There is no other word for that to me than tragedy. The Chinese culture is one that revolves firmly around family, and, in fact, family piety is a core tenant of Confucian philosophy. Each and every year, the largest human migration in the world happens during Chinese Spring Festival when millions of people board trains to get back home to their loved ones. It is a rite of passage that you must return to your family home. For many parents in China today, their lives completely revolve around their child, making sure he or she studies hard and gets into the best schools possible. Then there's that sort of unwritten obligation in China that once a child marries and has a baby of his own, it is the grandparents who will take care of the infant, even moving into the house when needed to make sure the baby's needs are met. The entire culture of China revolves around family. So what happens when you grow up in an orphanage and the realization finally hits that no one is ever going to choose you? Sadly, I have seen that many times it leads to great despair and depression, and many orphaned teens age out feeling quite lost and unsure of the future.

There have been so many times during my work where I have seen firsthand just how much these older kids ache for someone to love them completely. One of the most poignant came at a banquet we were hosting for orphaned teens we had helped through our education program. We were having such a great time, taking turns singing and sharing favorite foods and stories. At the end of the dinner, before everyone left, I stood up to toast all of the kids who were there. You should know that I am considered a terrible toaster in China because, while I know it is normally expected that you just say a few words, "To our friendship!" or "To your health," I am far too verbose. But it has always been done with the best of intentions because I want to make sure everyone understands just how much it means to me to get to spend time with them in China.

On this particular evening, I asked one of our Chinese directors to translate the toast for me. I'm sure she was thinking,

"Oh no, she's going to go long again," which I definitely did. I told each of the kids how very proud we were of them for their hard work, and I assured them that lots of people around the world were cheering them on and were committed to helping with their education. But then I used a word which I know far too many of us take for granted. I told the kids that I wanted them to know they were like FAMILY to us, and that we would be there for them to help them reach their dreams. It was supposed to be an innocent speech, and since we in America use that idiom all the time with people – "Hey, you're like family to me" – I didn't fully realize the weight my words would carry that night at dinner. The room went completely quiet, and several of the teens began to cry. As the orphanage director quickly hurried them all out, one of the older boys asked permission to stay and talk with me privately. We assured the director we would get him back to the orphanage very soon, and so they left us alone together in the large banquet room. I put my hand on his shoulder and asked him to tell me what was bothering him, and the teen simply dissolved into tears. I had 16- and 17-year-old sons myself at the time, and so I knew that is an age where some don't want to be mothered or touched, but I just couldn't help myself. I pulled him into a hug and held him for a long time while he sobbed against my shoulder. He told me there simply weren't words to describe the depth of his longing for a family. He kept repeating as I held him, "It's so hard to be alone. I would rather be dead than an orphan." As we sat and talked together, he told me that my toast had reopened the pain he had tried to lock away in his heart as a child when he realized no one wanted him as their son. What I had hoped would be a comfort to the kids, telling them "You are family to me," instead had reminded him of all he had lost out on as a child. The weight of his anguish settled deeply in my heart, and I suddenly understood that those of us who have grown up surrounded by caring families can never fully comprehend what it means to be orphaned. There is no way for us to fully grasp what it feels like to be all on your own as a child if we ourselves have not experienced it. I remembered the kids I had seen in orphanages with chicken pox, burning with fever while lying stoically all alone in their beds. I thought of those who are afraid of the dark or severe storms, trying to calm their pounding hearts by themselves since they know no parent will come to offer comfort. I can try my very best to understand what they live through, but the reality is that I grew up with very devoted parents, and so I have no way of fully knowing what it means to be that alone as a child.

We all have those moments in our lives when we have deep realizations of truth, don't we? I remember vividly the moment I realized that there was absolutely no difference between the love I felt for my biological kids and those who were adopted. My realization that love has nothing to do with genetics but everything to do with your heart was a wonderful truth to discover.

Not all truths bring joy, however. Some cause real sadness. But I believe all truths can bring a clearer understanding of life and deepen our mercy. I meet people all the time who say they can't even think about the fact that their adopted children ever lived in institutional care as it is just too painful to think of them being on their own. I struggled with that as well and didn't want to think about what my kids' lives were like as babies in an orphanage, even though I was working for LWB every day. It was easier to just push that to the back of my mind and concentrate on the material things the babies in our care needed: good formula, safe cribs, surgery assistance. But then my oldest daughter made me a grandmother, and I once again got to experience firsthand exactly what it is that a newborn baby truly wants and needs.

When my grandson Asher was born, I would have been happy to hold him up to my cheek all day long if I could, just breathing in his babyness. We truly lived to serve him, and to hear him cry even for a few minutes caused my heart pain. The moment he made noise, one of us jumped immediately into action to see what he needed. When he was hungry, he got fed. When he was tired, we rocked him to sleep with a lullaby. We spent hours gently talking to him, making eye contact, and letting him know that he was absolutely 100% cherished.

It was in my great love for my newborn grandchild, however, that I finally had to face the deep realization of what babies in orphanages completely miss out on, and what my own adopted kids had lived through as infants. Even with the most caring of nannies, the reality is that my children knew real hunger, true loneliness, and bewilderment and frustration when their cries for help went unanswered. They lived in a tiled room filled with babies and one lone woman trying her best to care for them all. When my son TJ came home through adoption, I would put him down for a nap in his bed. Very quickly, I realized that, when he woke up he would never make a sound. He would just lie there, for hours if I would have let him, staring at the ceiling because he had already learned in his life that no one would come if he cried. And so he would wake and stay silent, just staring at the ceiling. I would say to him, "TJ, make noise! I'll come right away if you just call out for me!" But no one had come for years, and so it took a long time for him to believe me. I remain in awe that most children who didn't have even their most basic of needs met can somehow open their hearts again to adults and learn to trust again. Their capacity to hold on to hope humbles me. I will never forget holding that 16-year-old boy in my arms as he wept, telling me how sad and afraid he felt in the orphanage and how much he still longed for a mother.

All around this world there are children growing up as orphans who deserve not only our compassion but our ACTION. There is so much pain in the world, but when we reach out and hold each other, there can be real healing as well. Whether it is a tiny newborn found abandoned on a cold winter's night or a young teen in an orphanage wishing she had a parent to talk to about the changes going on in her body, we all need someone next to us to let us feel safe and wanted. TJ taught me that lesson through two toy zebras he knew belonged together. "Baby... MOM." He took that realization into his heart and still treasures it to this day. I wish all of us could make a pledge that we would never take family for granted again when millions of orphaned children around the world would give anything to have one of their very own.

Fifteen

The Ethics of Orphan Care

"I'm not a doctor, but I play one on the Internet." That was the very bad joke that our volunteers and I started making as we began being asked daily whether or not we could provide help to yet another child abandoned with medical issues. We have a strong advisory board of physicians who review files for us and give us wonderful guidance and advice, but ultimately it often fell to me or our medical director to give the definitive message of, "Yes, let's operate" or "No, we aren't able to help." We have had to make that decision on whether or not to provide care thousands of times now. As the years went on in our work, however, we began to realize something very sobering. The children entering orphanage care in China began having an increasing number of medical needs, and so the decisions regarding their care were becoming more and more complex.

When I first began visiting Chinese orphanages in 2003, the rooms were filled with row after row of healthy baby girls abandoned due to the One Child policy introduced in 1978. Those of us in the adoption community had read everything we could find on the "whys" of female infant abandonment, and tens of thousands of healthy little girls were adopted by families around the world. Those children with medical issues I met back then had many of the special needs most commonly seen in children, such as cleft lip, VSD and ASD heart defects, missing limbs, and club feet. We did many "standard" surgeries during those first few years at LWB, and many of the kids could be healed with fairly straightforward operations.

But as every year passed, we saw the Chinese orphanage population begin to shift in major ways. Now it seemed as if every phone call we received was about a child found needing some sort of medical care, and China confirmed that trend when they released data saying that birth defects in their country had risen 70% in the last decade. One government official stated that birth defects now affected one in ten households in China, with a child being born every 30 seconds with a medical need. Current Chinese reports place the number of children being born with special needs each year at between one to three million, compared to the estimate by the March of Dimes that 120,000 babies are born with birth defects each year in the United States. One of the reasons cited for the marked increase in China is environmental pollution. The World Health Organization states that China is home to 16 of the world's dirtiest cities.

Sadly, with the increased rate of birth defects in China has also come a rise in the abandonment of children with medical needs. Orphanage directors now state that 95% or more of the children entering their care have some sort of special need, and very many of the kids have more than one medical issue requiring treatment. Whereas we used to be asked regularly to help babies with a single hole in their hearts, for example, we now are asked to help babies with up to five to eight heart diagnoses in their files. It amazes me how their bodies manage to survive when one tiny heart the size of a plum has single ventricle, complete endocardial cushion defect, single atrium, patent ductus arteriosus, and pulmonary stenosis. Or else we will accept a child into our medical program who we are told has a single need of anal atresia, for example, and then we will learn once we get him to the hospital that he also has a cleft palate, a heart defect, and multiple hernias.

This has made providing medical care to children in orphanages often very complex, and it made me learn the hard way that there are definite reasons why medical ethics committees are formed as making decisions for these children is often a very heavy weight to shoulder. It is made even more challenging when you realize you are "doing medicine" long distance and often relying on testing and reports done in very rural hospitals with outdated equipment. Add to that the differences which sometimes occur between Western and traditional Chinese medicine, coupled with language barriers and things lost in translation. The decisions on how to best move forward with medical care for a child are often not easy, and so many prayers for wisdom are lifted to heaven. The one thing that I have learned so clearly is that, when you are dealing with human life, there is no such thing as black and white decisions. And, rightly so, emotions run very high when you are talking about a child's life. But I have learned after doing this work for over a decade that there are often no simple answers as you try to figure out what is best for an extremely sick child living in institutional care.

There is, of course, that other part of doing medical charity work that so many people don't want to talk about, and that is the issue of funding. In a perfect world with green money trees everywhere, you could say to a hospital "Do everything possible to save her life regardless of cost," but, of course, that just isn't realistic for many charities who have "x" amount of dollars in the bank and who are trying to help as many kids as they can. Early on in this work, I began reaching out to other charities providing pediatric medical services to ask them how they handled these often very difficult decisions, and I learned that the policies varied greatly. For example, one doctor I spoke with told me that they had decided to only fund the simpler heart surgeries through their charity. Their board felt that doing ten less complex heart surgeries at $5,000 each was preferable to saving the life of one single child with severe heart disease at a cost of $50,000 or more. Other charities told me their policy was to heal the children "in the order of which they were received," regardless of cost, even if it meant helping less kids each year. Another said they tried to weigh which children had the best chance of actually being healed and triage the children accordingly.

Think about those situations for a moment and decide which one you feel is best. If you did indeed have a finite $50,000 in medical funding, how would you spend it? Would it go to the first child who crossed your path, regardless of the complexity of her medical needs, or would you try to use it for as many kids as possible? Let me make that even a bit harder for you. Imagine you have ten photos in front of you on a desk. Ten beautiful children's faces staring out at you, and it's on your shoulders to decide which of them get healing. Now you will understand why sometimes I sit in my office when our medical funds are running low asking myself if I really want to click "open" on the email photo attachment asking for medical help. Because if we can't raise the necessary funds, then I can picture exactly the child we are declining help. Sadly, it's definitely easier when you don't see their faces, even though the reality is that the written request in front of me is still a living, breathing child who needs assistance.

Not all decisions are about funding, however. I remember when an adoptive parent group reached out to us for help with a tiny baby girl who had a severe form of Beta Thalassemia. This is a blood disorder that reduces the production of hemoglobin in red blood cells, which is essential to carry oxygen to the body. Kids with this condition also often have life-threatening anemia, and this little girl clearly was struggling, with pale skin, weakness, and severe malnourishment. The parents who wrote me wanted to raise money immediately for a bone marrow transplant to save this little girl's life, which we had never attempted before in China. I began contacting specialists in both the U.S. and Hong Kong to get their opinions on whether a bone marrow transplant was even a viable option to save this child's life. We contacted a major children's hospital in southern China, who told us that it would cost between $25,000 and $50,000 US for the treatment – a staggering amount at that time in China. When I let the parent group know, I was immediately accused of putting a "price tag" on the life of a child, which was actually the furthest thing from my mind. I just wanted the parents to be realistic that any treatment planned for the little girl could not proceed without the funds being raised in advance since hospitals in China want the fees up front for procedures.

What we were investigating in this little girl's case, however, was the success rate of a transplant at that time in China as it was a fairly new procedure there for Thalassemia and was just starting to be done at more hospitals on the mainland. While many parents were writing me angry letters saying our only choice was to move forward immediately to save the baby's life, I was learning from doctors in Guangzhou and Hong Kong that only 10% of transplants at that time were successful. As an orphan, the little girl had no blood relatives to donate marrow to her, and so the odds of a successful match were very slim. One doctor in Guangdong I respected greatly told me quite bluntly, "You will probably kill her if you move forward with the procedure." And so there was the ethical dilemma we have faced so many times since. Do you move forward "no matter what" to try and save a child's life, even if moving forward has a high likelihood of ending her life immediately? But then how do you live with yourself if you decide not to provide medical care to a child who is so clearly sick? I do a lot of pacing as these decisions are made, and my worry over this little baby almost wore a groove in my floors.

We had another little girl come into our hands with a malignant brain tumor, and again I got very emotional letters pleading with me to get her treatment. Of course, as a mom myself, even discussing whether or not to provide care to a sick child hurts my heart deeply. I know it is very easy to get caught up in doing "everything possible" to save a child's life, but a friend once reminded me that we can never forget that it is the child who feels the pain of surgery; it is the child who is lying in the hospital; it is the child who endures the consequences of our decisions—always. For the type of brain cancer this little girl had, the cure rate in China was less than 6% at the time. And so the ethical question was raised of whether she should be put through opening her skull, intense chemotherapy, and radiation – all as an orphan with no parents to comfort her – if there was really little chance of a cure.

These are not easy decisions. These are terrible, horrible decisions that cause us to question ourselves again and again. But they are reality when you have a long waiting list of children needing to be healed who often require complex medical care which can't be provided to them locally. For the two little girls mentioned above, I am grateful to let you know that both ended up being adopted. The last I had heard, the little girl with Beta Thalassemia was doing very well, but sadly the little girl with brain cancer passed away shortly following her adoption. I took some comfort in knowing she had died with a loving family surrounding her, rather than lying alone in an orphanage crib.

Because of the complexity of special needs now being seen in Chinese orphanages, we often see medical conditions that many physicians in the U.S. rarely see in their own practices. I remember talking to my eye doctor once and having him tell me about a sad case he was working on with a three-year old girl. She had been diagnosed with retinoblastoma, a potentially deadly cancer which develops in the tissue of the eye. This is a very rare type of cancer, with only about 250 to 300 kids each year in the U.S. developing it. My doctor began explaining what it was to me when I stopped him to say we had treated about six kids with it through LWB in China. He was absolutely dumbfounded, telling me that none of his local colleagues had ever seen an actual case in person, and yet I had already seen six just in the orphanages we partnered with.

One of the first little boys we helped with this condition lived in a small orphanage in southern China. I liked this orphanage very much as the director treated the kids as if she was their mom, and all of the nannies I met from there seemed very loving and kind. The director contacted us when one of their babies, six-month-old Song, seemed to have a white spot on his eye. Tests confirmed that it was fast-growing retinoblastoma. The "good" thing about this type of cancer is that if it is diagnosed and treated early, it is highly curable. The terribly bad news, however, is that the eye often has to be completely removed to prevent the cancer from spreading to the brain or bone marrow. I still vividly remember discussing Song's case because it seemed unfathomable to me that we were going to tell a hospital to completely cut out a baby's eye. Most surgeries we did, of course, were to make a child "more whole," and yet we were making a decision to permanently blind a child in one eye. Yet, of course, it was for the greater good of saving his life, and so his right eye was removed. The first photos we got back of him were so difficult to see, but we gave thanks that his life was saved. For the next year, the updates we received on him said he was developing normally in every way. By 18 months he was running everywhere, and the nannies told us that he was an absolutely brilliant little boy whose language was exploding and who had a curiosity about life a mile wide.

A few months later, however, we got another phone call from his orphanage. They were worried that they could see a white spot in his remaining eye, and subsequent tests confirmed their fears. Little Song was one of the very rare cases where the cancer formed in both eyes. If you think making the decision to remove one eye from a child is a difficult one, you can imagine how very heartbreaking it is to consider making a child blind for life by removing the second. It doesn't matter if you know it will save his life; you still mourn and grieve that you are playing a part in making a child permanently blind.

The first time I met a child who was blind in an orphanage, my heart ached. The orphanage was crowded and loud, and she sat all day on her little chair against the back wall looking overwhelmed. I was told that her future would be difficult as she could not attend public school, and she would most likely never find work. The orphanage staff told me there was a good chance she would be institutionalized her entire life simply for not having sight. Other children with blindness I met were completely shut down in institutional care. For babies and children with sight who are confined to cribs most of their days, they can at least look around themselves. They can see other children or the ceiling or their nannies. But a child who is blind who is confined all day to a crib or a chair is even more likely to suffer from a lack of social, emotional, and cognitive stimulation required for normal development. I had sadly seen many such kids who actually developed "institutional autism" from the difficulties they experienced. And now we were being asked to give the green light to making Song blind as well. What if he wasn't adopted? Were we sentencing him to a life with no schooling? To a life permanently institutionalized? Of course, none of us wanted that for this amazing, vibrant little boy who was zooming around his orphanage and seeing well out of his one remaining eye. His life had to be saved, however, and so the message was sent to do surgery, causing Song's world to immediately be thrown into darkness.

The resiliency of children never ceases to amaze me. While Song lost his sight to retinoblastoma, his other senses became increasingly sharp, and his intelligence continued to bloom off the charts. I was so grateful that he was in such a supportive and caring orphanage as the nannies encouraged him to be as independent as he could. I had the honor to meet little Song in person right after his second birthday. I knew from his photos what a beautiful little boy he was, but meeting him face to face took my breath away. Even though he was just a toddler, he talked like a little adult. As soon as I walked in, he knew immediately that a stranger had come into his environment. "Who is that person?" he asked his nanny, even before they told him I was there. "Why is she here?" I had to keep reminding myself that the little boy in front of me was only TWO as he asked question after question, to the point that his orphanage director just laughed and said, "In case you haven't realized, this child is a genius." Oh yes, I had realized.

We had asked the orphanage right after his first surgery if they would please file his adoption paperwork, and they followed through and submitted his file to the national government. For months, no family stepped forward and so we began raising funds to offer a grant towards his adoption expenses. I was overwhelmed to see how many people were taken with this little boy's story of losing his eyes, and more and more people gave to his grant fund. At about the same time,

I became Facebook friends with an adoptive dad named Roy, who had messaged me about a little girl we were advocating for who had a limb difference like his daughter. He wrote: "These children know no limits. I see that in this child too. I do so hope that people looking at her adoption file will recognize this and not let her 'handicap' dissuade them!" I knew right then that I liked this man because he saw so clearly that a child's special needs should never define them.

Several months later, I got a Facebook message from Roy with a recent blog post attached that I had written about little Song. His note was short and to the point: "I can't believe I'm sending you this, but my wife and I think this is our son. Can you send more info?" I sat looking at my computer screen for a few moments before letting out a whoop of joy. He didn't say, "We are looking at a file of a child." He didn't say, "Can you tell me more about this boy?" Nope... he had written "We think this is our SON." I gave a prayer of thanks to God because I knew right then that little Song was going home. Now a few years later, I still thankfully get updates on this amazing child, who rides a scooter and goes to school and who has the vocabulary of a Harvard scholar. His future is limitless. Song reminds me that the weight of making terribly difficult decisions is worth everything when even one more child has his or her life transformed.

Another child who led us firmly down the path of ethical dilemmas was a baby from a rural orphanage in Anhui, who was born with an extremely complex heart defect which most likely led to her abandonment. She was just two months old when I first saw her, wrapped in a red orphanage blanket tied up tightly with an orange string. She had the most extraordinarily expressive dark eyes, and we gave her the Western name of Marisol. Her orphanage had called us when she developed severe pneumonia, and local doctors told us that she was too fragile to undergo testing to accurately diagnose her heart defect. Just a few weeks later, she went into severe respiratory distress; so we moved her to Shanghai with the hopes that the doctors at Fudan University would be able to help her.

The heart surgeons at Fudan are some of the very best in China. I can't say thank you enough to them for all of the children they have healed with their skills. They told us that Marisol needed immediate open heart surgery to survive, but they also cautioned us that it would be a very difficult operation. We told them to move forward, and we all waited through the night for news on how she had done. There was such an enormous feeling of joy when we learned she had survived the surgery and was resting in the ICU on a standard, post-op ventilator. If you've never seen a child who has had heart surgery, you should know that during the operation most kids are supported by a number of machines to help keep them alive. Ventilators can mechanically keep a child breathing since anesthesia often suppresses a body's natural urge to take breaths. One of the key pieces to a child doing well after a heart surgery is being weaned from the ventilator, and thankfully most kids can come off within a matter of days. It is pretty standard protocol that you want to remove a child from ventilation as quickly as you can because prolonged use leads to airway trauma, infection, and, of course, just the emotional toll which can come from being connected to a machine.

Sometimes, however, when the doctors go to disconnect the ventilator, a child is unable to breathe normally on her own. Their oxygen levels fall critically low, and their heart rate increases; so the decision is quickly made to keep them on ventilation and try again in a few days. The first time the hospital tried to wean Marisol from her breathing machine, she immediately began to struggle, and so doctors told us she needed more time. One week went by, then two, and each time they would try again she would be unable to come off of ventilation. Soon a month had passed, and then six weeks, and tiny Marisol remained in the hospital connected to hoses and machines. Being in the ICU in China is a very expensive situation, just like it is in the United States. One difference however is that family members are not allowed in the ICUs in China, and so anyone who is critically ill has no loved ones surrounding them. Of course, Marisol was an orphan and had no parents to soothe and comfort her, but because she was in the ICU it meant that there couldn't be an orphanage nanny with her either. She was connected to machines being cared for by nurses whose shifts would change every 12 hours. Each and every day we would ask for an update on this beautiful little girl, and each and every day we were told, "She is unable to breathe on her own." And so what do you do? At what point do you remove life support for an orphaned child? At what point do you have to face the reality that the rapidly increasing medical bills are far exceeding the kind donations given by your supporters? No one wants to make that decision, I can assure you. Every time we discussed her case, we would end the call by saying, "Let's give her one more day."

On day 60 of Marisol being on the ventilator, we knew the odds of her ever being weaned were very slim. The medical funds we had raised for her had long been used up, and we were now using general funds to keep life support going. The hospital had agreed to cut their costs substantially as well, but we all knew this couldn't be a never-ending treatment. Obviously a decision had to be made, but honestly none of us wanted to make it. After many phone calls back and forth, we decided we would give Marisol one more week to breathe on her own, while praying nonstop that somehow she would miraculously be able to do just that on the final try. On the morning of day 66, doctors at Fudan slowly removed her breathing tube while checking her vitals carefully, and that amazing baby girl somehow began breathing normally on her own. I think you could have heard my scream of joy two states over, and from that point forward she was known as Mighty Marisol, the little girl who had beaten the odds and who had somehow found the strength inside of her to keep fighting for another day.

During Marisol's summer long hospital stay, I had called my good friend Dr. Joyce Hill many times, asking her how you know when it's time to let go. She told me something which I have carried in my heart ever since. She said, "You never let go. You keep fighting for that child until they draw their last breath." But she went on to explain that the reality is that sometimes a child is simply too sick to be healed on this earth, and that I needed to remember that we can fight for them simply by holding them and offering comfort, and, of course, by praying for them continually. Joyce and her husband have several units in China which offer palliative care to children, but, of course, everyone doing this work struggles to know when it is time to continue putting a child through more and more medical procedures and when it is time to let a child pass with love and dignity.

There is no black and white, and I know now that anyone who wants to armchair quarterback these decisions probably has never done this heart-wrenching work themselves. These are children's lives we are being asked to make decisions for, and every child's life is priceless to me. When we are faced with cases of children who are extremely sick and complex, we gather all the information we possibly can from medical experts and then ask God to help us in making the wisest and most compassionate decisions possible. We also ask for strength and comfort for our own hearts as well when those decisions are more than any of us want to bear.

Sixteen

Healing Homes

One of the things we learned pretty quickly in working with really sick children is that in many cases you can't just "do a surgery" and then discharge a child directly back to an orphanage. I will, with much regret, say that we learned this the hard way, after watching several children we had helped with heart surgeries develop life-threatening chest infections when they returned to orphanages to lie flat in cribs all day. Anyone who has been through surgery themselves knows that you need a dedicated caregiver following most operations. In many crowded orphanages, that just isn't possible. Additional ethical questions were raised for us on whether you should ever do surgery on a child, even one who is dying, if you can't be assured that adequate post-op care will be available to them. We knew that in order to solve these issues, we needed a safe place for them to go after their surgeries. We envisioned a transitional unit where kids could go for nurturing care after their hospitalization before returning to their home orphanages after they were considered fully healed.

In 2006, thanks to our friends the Hills, we were offered a large room inside the Hope Foster Home outside of Beijing to create a nine-bed "step-up, step-down" unit for medically fragile children. We decided we needed the "step-up" part as well as we had sent many babies directly from orphanages to the hospital who arrived too thin and malnourished to undergo major surgery. Our new medical unit at Hope would be a welcoming place for babies to both prepare for their operations and then recover post-surgery. We decided to call the unit "Heartbridge," as we wanted it to be a bridge to health for all the children we sent there. It was such a beautiful room, with red homemade quilts and sunshine streaming through the windows, and almost instantly it was full of children, with a waiting list of kids also needing a bed.

In 2007, I told Joyce and Robin that we simply couldn't keep up with the medical requests we were getting from orphanages due to a lack of post-op bed space, and they generously agreed to give us a second room to bring Heartbridge up to 18 beds. I could write an entire book on the stories of the kids who have gone through the arms of Heartbridge nannies as every single one of them is a miracle to me, especially since most arrived in such fragile states.

One Heartbridge story started with a little boy we called Max, who was from a rural orphanage several provinces over from Beijing. At the time, we were doing a lot of medical work in his city, and the local orphanage director had called us about a newborn baby they had found with anal atresia, a life-threatening condition which often requires surgery within the first 48 hours of life. Many babies with this condition are given temporary colostomies, a surgical procedure that brings one end of the large intestine out through an opening in the child's abdominal wall. The opening (a stoma) is where a baby's body waste will be expelled into a cloth or plastic bag which is sealed to the skin and changed when needed. Babies with colostomies need extremely vigilant care, and five-pound Max found himself with one in order to save his life. We knew there was no way we could send him back to the orphanage in his condition; so he came to live with us at Heartbridge following his operation. I was so thankful he was in our hands as he developed severe pneumonia with a dangerously high fever and racing heart soon after the surgery. We were able to get him immediately back to the hospital for treatment. I don't know that he would have survived if he had been back at the orphanage instead.

Several months after Max came to Heartbridge, Arlene Howard, one of our volunteers from the U.K., was visiting his birth city. Before going to see the LWB foster families whom she had come on the trip to visit, she was asked by the orphanage director if she would like to see the new building they were using for government sponsored "family care." They had purchased several apartments and had hired nannies to keep six to eight kids in each, allowing them to experience more of a home life versus living in an institution. When Arlene walked into the first apartment, she immediately saw an infant baby who was far too thin. He had been born with cleft lip, and it was obvious that he wasn't able to feed well because of it, and every tiny rib showed in his chest. I still remember the first photo I saw of him which was taken during her visit as he looked so very gaunt and weak.

Arlene told the staff she would get cleft bottles and better formula for the little boy, but then things took an incredible turn. One of the nannies turned to Arlene and mentioned that the malnourished baby possibly had a twin. When Arlene asked where the other baby was, she was told that we had already moved him to Beijing! Max, the little boy with the colostomy who had been at Heartbridge for three months by that time, had a possible twin brother who was now struggling for his very life 400 miles away. When the orphanage director had originally called asking us to help Max, he never mentioned that a second baby had been found the exact same day. Now when I think about these wonderful boys, I always thank God that Arlene was asked to go to the apartment that day. What if she wouldn't have had time? Or what if the invitation had never been extended? I know without a doubt that her seemingly coincidental visit to that small apartment saved not only the little boy's life but also permanently reunited him with his twin.

We made immediate plans to move this baby with cleft to Heartbridge as well, and the first photos we have of the boys together are like Mutt and Jeff. Max, after having three months of TLC and good formula at Heartbridge, was a total butterball, while his twin, Matthew, who had struggled since birth with getting enough to eat, was almost half his size. We were bound and determined to catch the boys up to each other just as quickly as we could. We also ordered a DNA test for the boys and waited anxiously for the results. They came back showing that Max and Matthew were indeed twins, which thankfully allowed us to insist that they be submitted for adoption together. They are twin brothers forever now, having been adopted by a family in America, thanks to a nanny who dared to speak up that day.

Because so many orphaned babies with cleft struggle to eat, we kept brainstorming on more and more ways to help this vulnerable population of children. It was just so heartbreaking to think that any child would pass away from being born with cleft lip, and I kept remembering Dr. Padilla's challenge to us back in 2004 on our first cleft trip to "Dream big, dream big." By 2007, it had become clear to us that we needed to open a specialized medical unit just for their care. Cleft is one of the most common special needs in China, and so we knew we wouldn't have any trouble ever filling the beds. We approached officials at the national level soon after with our proposal for a "cleft care center," and they gave us their full approval with one small stipulation. Rather than using the word "center," they asked that we call our project an LWB "cleft healing home" instead. They liked the thought that orphaned babies would be cared for in a warm and safe home environment versus a more clinical sounding one. We, of course, readily agreed to the language change, and, in the spring of 2008, the Anhui Cleft Healing Home opened its doors.

One of our first residents was eight-month-old Tyler, who traveled 14 hours by bus with his orphanage nanny for the individualized care that he needed for his cleft. It was such a long journey, with their bus breaking down twice, and, when he arrived to the home, we immediately had to rush him to the hospital as he had pneumonia, dehydration, and severe malnutrition. He weighed just six pounds at eight months of age. Bless the nanny who agreed to bring him such a long way as she literally helped save his life. Over the next few years, over 120 babies with cleft came to our Anhui home, and each one was as precious as the next.

We began hearing from the public, though, since pictures of babies with cleft were now on our website and blog almost daily, that some people didn't want to see children with this unrepaired special need. Many said it made them feel uncomfortable and that they would have to cover up the photo in order to look at our website. I still hear from people occasionally today who say they just can't look at these photos, but to me the only way we can ever get over a stigma surrounding a special need is to bring it out into the open. I completely understand that seeing children who haven't received medical care can hurt one's heart, but I also know that the more you look – the more you REALLY look – you come to see that every child is absolutely beautiful exactly as they are. I love the huge wide smiles of babies with bilateral cleft, their eyes twinkling when they grin, and I would just encourage anyone who struggles when seeing kids who look differently to not turn away. How wonderful it is when you start to see every child you meet with your heart, rather than just your eyes.

Over the last decade, LWB has run healing homes in many Chinese provinces, and we have seen our homes adapt to the changing orphanage populations by now accepting babies with almost every medical need. Our homes are one of the most rewarding projects I have ever had the honor to be involved with. They literally save lives each day, and there is just no way for me to even describe how much that humbles me to get to play even a small part. To know we have facilities now where we can immediately move babies who are critically ill is a dream come true, and the children who have come through the doors of our homes have stretched my heart in ways I never could have imagined. The strength of the children who have come into our hands simply astounds me as they overcome obstacles which often seem insurmountable.

I remember one December right before Christmas when we were called by a rural orphanage in central China that had just discovered a tiny newborn left outside their gates. Obviously born far too soon, little Qian weighed less than two pounds. While we can never know for sure, since she wasn't left with a note from her birth parents, from what I knew about fetal development, there is a chance she was only about 28 weeks along when her mom gave birth. Even as I was making note of her information, I was looking up the temperature in her hometown that night, and my heart became heavy when I saw that it was a frigid 14 degrees, one of the coldest nights of the year.

If your baby is delivered at 28 weeks in the United States, you are going to have an entire neonatology team to help, including doctors, nurses, respiratory therapists, and more. As the baby is born, the team would closely monitor all body functions, including heart rate and oxygen levels, and sometimes a breathing tube would be used to help the newborn breathe. The tiny infant might be given specialized drugs to help keep her lungs expanded, and, of course, warmth and more warmth as she would be placed in an incubator which would keep constant track of her vitals. But for Qian, born on that cold December night, instead of the safety of a hospital she was wrapped in a scrap of cloth and then left alone outside in the frigid darkness. Miraculously, somehow, she found the strength to hold on until she was found and the orphanage could call us for help. They told us she was dark blue and that her tiny arms felt like ice. We rushed her urgently to the nearest hospital with a pediatric ICU, where she was diagnosed with hypothermia and prematurity in a true fight for her life. For the next two months, she spent her days inside an incubator. Since her immune system had not developed before she was born, she fought infection after infection. And yet she persevered. Eight weeks after she was found, baby Qian discharged to our Heartbridge Healing Home weighing a whopping 4.5 pounds. There she simply thrived, being held and hugged by our nannies. Soon after she graduated from our home, the very picture of health, she was chosen by a local Chinese family for adoption.

Another baby who beat all the odds against him was a boy we named Little Joe (yes, we always used both names just like on "Bonanza"). Little Joe was born with a condition known as gastroschisis, which is a medical need that makes you say, "OH MY GOODNESS," the first time you see it.

You might already know that in humans the small intestine is about 20 feet long and the large intestine is about five feet long. But it is all folded perfectly and tucked safely behind our abdominal walls; so we just take that awe-inspiring fact for granted... until a baby is born with an incomplete abdominal wall and with the intestines on the outside of the body. If you type "gastroschisis" into your search engine and hit "images," Little Joe's story becomes even more extraordinary.

In the U.S., just like with Qian, if a mother gave birth to a child with this condition, an entire team of medical professionals would make sure the intestines were protected and that surgery could take place as quickly as possible. Sadly, Little Joe was abandoned shortly after his birth, and, even more tragically, he was left in a location where he wasn't discovered quickly. By the time someone did find him, his intestines had been exposed to the elements and parts had dried out. I'm sure you don't need me to tell you that is never a good thing.

As soon as the receiving orphanage called us, we rushed him to the hospital, where doctors immediately wrapped his organs with a moist plastic bag. Since his intestines had been outside of his body for so long, first in the amniotic fluid of the womb and then outside in the air, doctors decided that they needed to very slowly put them back into their proper position. For the next month, Little Joe was in an incubator with his intestines in a plastic bag literally hanging above him. Little by little, each day they would lower more of it into his abdomen. Once it was all where it was supposed to be, they finally were able to surgically close his belly, and Little Joe came to live in one of our healing homes, weighing in at a respectable eight pounds.

Little Joe's sunny personality shone through the moment he came through the doors of the home. He started grinning almost immediately, and he would giggle and wave at anyone who came near. I would smile each week as I got his reports, which repeatedly said, "This baby is more outgoing and smart than other children his age." He absolutely loved interacting with his nannies, and he was so quick to learn how to hug and give kisses. It was almost like he somehow knew he wasn't supposed to survive this life, and so he had become a baby who was going to grasp it with both hands as if to say, "World, I am HERE!"

Without specialized healing home care, I know Little Joe wouldn't be here today, and I give thanks continually that God has brought us together with all the right people in China to keep this program running so beautifully. My dream is that someday there will be specialized healing homes in every Chinese province as the need for intensive, one-on-one care for orphaned children continues to increase with the rise in the abandonment of babies born with medical needs.

When I was in my 20s, one of the wisest ministers I ever knew gave a sermon called "Compassion Over Judgment." He reminded us that it is so very easy to quickly judge people and to feel that the way we do things is better than theirs. Most everyone does it multiple times each day even though we seldom know the full story of another person's life and all they have lived through. The reality is that we have no way of knowing the pain the people we meet might carry in their hearts. Instead of blind judgment, he challenged us to pour out compassion to those we meet instead; to let our words and thoughts heal, rather than wound. He said it could be life-changing if we could make that subtle shift in our thinking, and I have tried to live by those three words as much as I possibly can ever since. I have repeated "compassion over judgment" so many times in my mind as I have done this work as I have come to realize that I honestly knew so little about what it is really like to try and care for so many children with often limited resources.

I can give a really quick example of how we often don't fully understand orphanage care as Westerners with a simple story about the bamboo mats and wooden boards that many orphanages use in their baby cribs. I sometimes get emails from parents in the West upset to learn that their kids slept on wooden slats instead of a soft mattress while they were in institutional care. We are often asked by adoptive parents to buy bedding for orphanage cribs, and this is a classic example of not always knowing the whole picture of institutional care, especially if there are limited nannies. I remember being shocked myself the first time I saw babies sleeping on boards because we all want infants to be surrounded by softness, but then a really kind nanny I trusted greatly told me that it was actually for the babies' benefit. She explained that they had tried cotton mattresses many years before, but since the babies' thin cloth diapers leaked continually, the mattresses soon became soaked with urine. They couldn't easily wash them as they were in a southern, humid climate, and, when they had tried, the mattresses had just molded instead. The nannies hated seeing the babies lying in urine, and they felt it was far cleaner and more sanitary for the infants to sleep on boards and bamboo mats, which could be quickly washed down in the event of an accident. Yes, it might have looked stark and even uncaring to a foreigner, but the decision had been made out of a real concern for the babies' well-being. The nannies were doing the best they could with the resources they had at that time. Compassion over judgment.

I know that is a really simplified example, but I have thought a lot about those three words as I have worked with our healing homes program and have seen children come to us malnourished, covered with diaper rash sores, or wracked with infection. How could anyone allow this to happen? In the beginning, I honestly felt anger. But then I came to deeply understand just how difficult it is to care for so many babies at once who are often extremely sick and fragile. I finally understood just how long it can take to feed a baby with a cleft who doesn't have a good sucking reflex, and I began talking with nannies in orphanages about the difficulties they now face having to act basically as nurses instead of simple caregivers.

I remember going into an orphanage in far western China that was extremely poor. The infants were lined up two to three to a crib, and, as we talked to the director, she explained that every single one of the children was in need of medical assistance. We walked past cribs with babies who had spinal tumors, cleft lip, heart defects, massive hernias, and more. We stopped by a crib against the far wall that held two tiny babies with cleft. One of the little boys was so weak that I could see he was trying to cry in hunger, but no sound came out of his mouth. He just turned his head side to side with his mouth open, silently gasping. I immediately asked if they had cleft bottles for him. The nannies told us they didn't even know what cleft bottles were; so we ran down to the van to get some for them. I will admit that my heart was hurting so much for the little boy, and I was on my way to thinking the orphanage didn't care about him very much to let him get to that state. But as we went back to the baby room and explained how to use the squeezie bottle, his nanny got tears in her eyes as she felt such relief. She then proceeded to tell me that nothing had worked when feeding the tiny boy. They had tried normal bottles with no luck, and had even tried an eyedropper filled with formula, but he continued to lose weight. My jaw just about dropped on the floor when she reached over and grabbed a long piece of yellowed rubber tubing and then shared with me that the only way they could get food into his stomach was for her to thread the rubber tube down his throat and then carefully pour formula into him. This was not a medical quality NG tube but just a small piece of hosing they had bought locally. They had been so frantic about the little boy getting weaker and weaker that they had resorted to drastic homemade measures to try and keep him from dying. Those three words from my minister poured over me once again: compassion over judgment. We took little Scotty (as he came to be known) into one of our healing homes, where he quickly regained his full health. One of his early photos after he came to stay with us is one I look at frequently as he has this enormous grin on his face from ear to ear as if he is saying, "Life with a full belly is mighty fine."

The other part of doing this work where I think it is essential to practice compassion over judgment is with nannies in orphanages who sometimes appear to be distant or aloof. I am not saying that there aren't some really bad apples out there, as, of course, there are uncaring people the world over. But this is one area which is much more complex to me now that I know the realities of working with really sick children. We have had thousands of kids come through our medical program over the years, and hundreds have stayed with us in our healing homes. We, of course, want every one of our nannies to pour themselves into a child, and we want them to love those kids as if they were their own. That is how it should be in an ideal world, right? And miraculously we have that with so many of the nannies we employ. But I have learned the hard way that losing a child whom you love takes a very real piece of your heart away. And while those wounds begin to heal with time, that missing piece remains. The loss of that child remains real. With orphanage nannies and the nannies in our healing homes, who are now working with very sick children at times, they face loss continually. There is the loss they feel when saying goodbye to a child through adoption, but that is one they can understand is ultimately a joy as that child is going on to a full life with a family. However, they also have to face loss through the pain of death when a child's illness finally takes them from this world. How many of us have had to watch a child take her last breath right in front of us? Nannies of children born with medical needs have to face that far too often, and it never gets any easier. I think about what we are asking our team members in China to do all the time and how working with us has caused many of them at very young ages to face the death of children, something many people in this world thankfully never have to experience in person.

Many years ago, we had a baby girl with cleft and heart disease in one of our healing homes who had the Western name of Kate. At the time, our home manager was a young, unmarried woman who was amazing with the kids. She fully invested herself into each of their lives, and in all the photos she sent she would have a baby in her arms, looking so contented. Kate was such a tiny little thing when she came into our hands. She arrived to us malnourished and was examined by our doctor, who said that, with careful feeding and nurturing, she would most likely recover. One night, about a month after she arrived, however, her nanny went to get her and saw that Kate was deep blue. She quickly got our home manager, and the two of them raced to the hospital with their hearts pounding, trying desperately to get the tiny baby to breathe. Our manager held Kate in her arms and was frantically trying to resuscitate her, but the baby was in complete respiratory distress. Right as they pulled up to the hospital, Kate took her last breath and then lay perfectly still in our manager's arms. She had died just 20 feet from the hospital doors. The shock and grief over losing baby Kate was immense. Her death shook everyone at the home, and no one could mention the little baby's name without the tears beginning again. Several nannies said they couldn't continue to do the work as it was just too painful to lose a child whom they had personally held in their arms. And yet this is what we ask nannies in orphanages to do every single day. We expect them to pour out love on the children in their care, and then have those kids leave through adoption to the U.S. or Europe, most likely never to see them again, or to love a child with often complex medical needs who has the real risk of dying far too soon. And, frequently, as fast as a child leaves an orphanage, there is another entering to take his place. There is often no time to fully process one's grief and sorrow before the nonstop work begins again. Attach... love... loss... grief. Attach... love... loss... grief. It takes so much from your heart.

I now know that there is actually a name for this experience: compassion fatigue. The official definition is an extreme state of stress experienced by those helping people in often highly traumatic circumstances, but I have come to realize it basically means "loving until it hurts." There are lots of symptoms of compassion fatigue, but one of them is shutting off part of your heart to feeling again after it has been broken again and again through loss. I of course can't say that every nanny in an orphanage suffers from this condition, but I am sure many of them do, even if they can't fully put words to it. After living through the loss of so many babies myself over the years, and after wanting to help certain kids so badly but then having to realize that some just can't be healed, I understand that some caregivers have to steel their hearts against additional pain or else they would destroy themselves emotionally. This is heartbreaking work at times, and everyone has to deal with it in their own way to survive. I am amazed at how many nannies can say goodbye again and again to the children they love and yet still throw open their arms to the next. These are women who are paid minimum wage and who often work long shifts of 24 hours or more. They are women who have told me they wish they could do more for the kids but who often don't have the resources. They most definitely deserve compassion over judgment in so many situations. Again, I am not a Pollyanna and recognize that there are some nannies working in orphanages who definitely shouldn't be caring for kids, but I also have a deeper understanding now of just how hard it can be to work with so many children who have such a wide variety of needs. I know the grief I have personally gone through saying goodbye to the kids in our programs who have lost their battles to illness. While I have held many of them in my arms on my trips to China, just as many have died with me only knowing them through photos and reports, and yet the pain is still immense. It is a sorrow so deep that it is hard to take a breath.

Very early in my work, one of our volunteers in Ireland, Julie Flynn, suggested I should light a candle for the babies we mourn, to have a tangible way to say goodbye. For the last ten years, I have done this ritual late at night, honoring the children who are gone far too soon with a tiny flame against the darkness. I always feel like I have failed in some way, even when I know the sad reality that, despite our best efforts, some children simply can't survive. I know that so many of the women working in orphanages across the world feel the same sorrow and guilt when they are unable to fully help those in their care.

If you ever get to meet a nanny in an orphanage or in one of our healing homes, make sure to smile and say thanks for all they are trying to do. They are so often overlooked. The women in China who genuinely open their hearts to hurting children deserve to be honored and celebrated. The work they are doing is profound.

Seventeen

Aging Out

As I have mentioned earlier, the fateful age for orphaned children in China is 14 – as it is on that birthday that they are no longer allowed to be legally adopted and must begin making plans for what their lives will look like when they finally leave the walls of the orphanage. There is a lot of misinformation out there about what happens to these kids once they "age out." I frequently see websites which insinuate that every orphaned child in China will end up in the sex trade or on the streets someday, and that simply isn't true. The majority of orphanages we work with try their very best to help kids find their way, with some providing small apartments and funding for vocational school or higher education for those who have shown a desire to make better lives for themselves. Of course, every teen is a unique individual and every orphanage has their own policies in place; so making sweeping generalizations about the outcome of those who age out is impossible. I can only go off of my own experiences with the young people we have been involved with, and I have seen repeatedly that even those who are smart and outgoing can face very big obstacles when they leave government care. Deep and ingrained stigmas surrounding those who have been abandoned in China remain, and there are still many schools and companies which believe it would be unlucky to have an orphan in their midst. Many institutionalized children, for example, are only able to attend the lowest level public schools as parents who are paying often high fees for the better schools don't want their children attending with kids who are deemed "undesirable." When you combine going to one of the lowest tier schools with not having a devoted parent pushing you to do homework and try harder in your studies, you often see young teens in orphanages who only have rudimentary educations and who have trouble believing their lives will ever be better.

Now that I have worked in China for so long, I have seen a generation of kids who grew up in orphanage care have to step out on their own. Kids that I met when they were just five or six are now in their late teens, and those I met when they had already aged out of the adoption process are now firmly adults, with such a wide variety of outcomes. They deserve to have their stories told because I don't think many of them fully realize just how much they have accomplished and overcome.

One of the first older girls I met in China was a teen named Lin. I felt an immediate connection with her when I learned that she had helped to take care of my daughter Anna when she was still a baby in the orphanage. She was 15 the first time I met her, and she had this amazing smile which lit up her face and let you know immediately the kindness of her heart. Lin had a medical condition known as vitiligo, a skin disease which causes the body to lose pigment in sometimes very large areas. People with vitiligo often have white patches on their body, and it can impact the skin, hair, and sometimes even eyes. It is not life-threatening and is not contagious. But without a doubt, vitiligo can be life-altering, especially in cultures where visible special needs are not readily accepted. People with this condition often develop low self-esteem or even begin withdrawing from others, and yet Lin did not. When I met her the first time, her eyes were literally dancing with laughter. She firmly tucked her arm into mine to show me around the orphanage.

It was clear in speaking with her for only a few moments that this was a young lady with a powerfully intelligent mind; a teen who was making a conscious choice to look forward to her future. Like all orphaned children, though, she had suffered tremendous grief in her childhood. Her parents had died when she was very young, and she was taken to live with a relative who kept her until age six, before being relinquished to the local orphanage. Such enormous loss for a young girl.

As I got to know Lin better during the next few years, I discovered that she dreamed of being a teacher someday. She was so gifted with younger kids and was so enthusiastic and smart that I knew immediately this would be a perfect calling for her. We told Lin that if she continued to study hard, we would pay for her to go to a local teacher college. A piece of cake for someone so smart and outgoing, right? Sadly, I quickly learned that getting accepted to college with white patches on your arms and face at that time was far more difficult than I ever could have imagined.

One of the directors at Lin's orphanage began helping her make applications to the local schools, but time after time he would be told that they refused to accept her since she looked "so scary" with her white skin. Principals would literally tell him that she would frighten the other students so they would be unable to concentrate and study, and I would silently scream to the heavens when hearing this because Lin was so beautiful and lovely. She just happened to have a little bit less melanin in some places than other people. Was that really going to stop her from obtaining her dream of being a teacher? However, knowing that almost everything in life has a price connected to it, we just decided to keep upping ours. Thankfully, we only had to go up a few hundred dollars more in "bonus tuition" before one of the local schools saw the light and accepted Lin into their class. And boy did she work hard, studying nonstop to prove that she deserved to be there and earning the highest marks possible.

When it was time for her to graduate, I felt like a mother hen who had successfully launched one of her chicks out of the nest. I was certain that Lin would become a respected teacher in the city and that she could go on to whatever life she wanted to build for herself. After all, she was smart, hardworking, and, in my mind, absolutely beautiful. I quickly learned, yet again, that finding a job in the local community with such a visible, albeit minor, special need was going to prove next to impossible. Once again, we were told that she was too scary to be hired on as a teacher. One principal of a school where she had sent a job application sat right across from her and said, "Surely you can understand that you would frighten all of the students with the way you look. No parent would pay money to have a teacher looking like you do." How do you hear those ignorant words again and again and yet still maintain your self-esteem and pride? Those are terrible, hurtful words… and yet somehow Lin refused to give in.

At the time, we were running an orphanage school in the very institution where she had grown up, and I will admit that a part of me felt like we would have somehow failed Lin if we were unable to get her a job in the "outside" world. It became clear, however, that the local schools, which charged parents often very high fees, were never going to agree to hire someone who looked different, and so we offered Lin a teaching job at our school. I was very glad when she agreed, and I soon realized that having her as a teacher in the orphanage had so many incredible benefits for the kids in her class. Lin understood better than anyone the emotional issues her tiny students had gone through. She understood abandonment and loss, having lived through it herself. Whenever an older child was brought to the orphanage by the police, she would be the first one to try and sooth their fears and explain where they were going to be living. She understood that everyone needs someone in their corner fighting for them, and so she became a fierce advocate for all the kids in her class, regardless of their special needs. The school principals who couldn't look past the white patches on her skin lost out on the best teacher they could have ever hired, but the kids in the orphanage gained an absolutely extraordinary mentor and friend.

Lin now has her own apartment, and she even saved up enough money to purchase a bright red motor scooter to ride to and from the orphanage each day. Sadly, it was stolen one night. When I told her how sorry I was, she looked at me with those same mirth-filled eyes and told me that she has had so many blessings in her life and people believing in her dreams that she couldn't mourn a possession. One summer, I got to spend a week with her traveling through western China. Whenever she would look at me and laugh with such joy at the things we were seeing, I would stop and wonder how one individual can experience loss and inequity in life and become bitter, while another, like Lin, can have everything bad thrown their way and yet still choose joy. For that is what Lin has done, despite all of the injustices and even malice shown her. She has chosen joy, and that has impacted my own life in a huge way as well. Now when I find myself starting to grumble about something, I think of Lin and remind myself that, while we can't control the way the world views us, we absolutely can control whether we let others tear us down. I have learned so many powerful life lessons through the children I have met in orphanages, and I try to carry their wisdom in my heart each day.

Another young woman I respect and admire greatly also grew up in an orphanage in southern China. Her story was a very difficult one. She was actually from Shandong Province, far to the north, but, when she was just a little girl, her father put her on a long distance bus, telling her they couldn't keep her any longer and that she needed to be quiet and good. Ming said she was more afraid than she had ever been in her life, and she sat in the back of the bus silently crying until it arrived in southern China 15 hours later. After all the passengers debarked, the bus driver told her she had to get off as well, and she barely remembers stumbling off and then beginning to aimlessly walk, with no idea of what she was supposed to do. She doesn't remember if it was hours or days later when a policeman found her, and then she was taken to the local orphanage to live.

Ming took her father's last words to heart, and she remained a quiet little girl who always tried to be good for the orphanage nannies. When I first met her, she was eight years old. I was introduced to her because she had become very sick. Her face was extremely pale. I was told that she had begun vomiting blood each day, but no one could figure out what was going on with her. I was in her town that day to help arrange heart surgery for several babies in her orphanage, but, as soon as I heard what was happening with Ming, we offered to move her immediately to the hospital for testing. Ming quietly asked me how many babies in the orphanage needed heart surgery to live. When I said there were four infants needing help, she said I needed to promise that they would all be healed first before any funds would be spent on her. We told her that was irrelevant; that her life was just as important as the babies. But she shook her head emphatically and said she wouldn't be able to live with herself if she thought money spent on her would stop a baby from getting surgery. She refused to even discuss it further until we assured her that all the kids in her orphanage who needed medical help would get it. She was just eight years old, and she had been let down by so many adults in her life at that point. Yet she wanted all the other children to get help before she did. She didn't have any possessions or money, but to me this was perfect charity, touching me to the core. *"Help the babies first."* This was her heartfelt plea. At the tender age of eight, she already had a true mother's heart, even though her own mom had disappeared from her life forever.

As Ming grew up, we also promised to help her go to college if she studied hard, and I was thrilled to learn that she had chosen nursing for her career. Like Lin, she excelled in her classes, and she now works in an orphanage as a full-time nurse. The staff there told me that she is always tender and gentle with the children in her care, managing to start IVs and give immunizations without causing any tears. She has found her life's work, and she does it very well. Neither Lin nor Ming has ever had a boyfriend, which is often a very difficult thing for orphaned adults as many marriages in China are arranged due to family connections and what one can financially bring to the table. Few mothers-in-law would be open to having an orphan join their family, but I still keep praying that someday they will meet kind young men who will see them for the lovely and generous people they are. They would both make the most amazing wives and mothers. If that can't happen for them in the current social climate, then I'm still grateful that they get to use their compassion and their gifts to impact the lives of a younger generation of orphaned children. Lin and Ming have both chosen joy, despite having heard repeatedly that they were unworthy of it.

LWB has been honored to help many orphaned teens go on to fulfill their dreams of attending college, and each one who has found their way makes my heart glad. I still worry greatly, however, about whether the world will treat them kindly. I was once told that those kids who are "true" orphans, meaning their parents were killed, are actually more accepted than those who were abandoned as that is a stigma which is very difficult to overcome. As a mom who has parented six teens so far, I know what an emotional period adolescence is, and so I worry about who is helping to guide them through the myriad of feelings and emotions which are inevitable during this period of life. Who is talking to the teens in orphanages about the very real topics of puberty and staying safe? I found out that in many places there wasn't a lot of discussion going on at all, which made me very nervous as I knew that children starved for physical and emotional connections could often make very bad choices as they hit their teenage years.

Those fears were confirmed one day when I got an email about a missing teen in one of the orphanages where we worked. Fang was a very pretty but shy young lady, with dimples on both sides of her cheeks which I had only been blessed to see a few times when she thought I wasn't looking. The email said that Fang had not come home from school the day before, and everyone in the orphanage was panicked wondering where she had gone. The orphanage staff searched everywhere for her, and finally they were able to convince a few of her classmates to admit that they had seen her leave school with an older man. My heart immediately fell, but there was nothing I could do except pray she would be found safely. A week went by, and then two, with no word at all on Fang's whereabouts. Sixteen days after she first disappeared, Fang returned to the orphanage with bruises on her arms and in complete shock. She was pale and sweating, and her hands were shaking uncontrollably. The orphanage doctor put her to bed, where she refused to speak for many more days. One of the older girls in the orphanage finally was able to coax her to talk about where she had been, and Fang told her story through tears. She explained that a man had struck up a conversation with her one day on the way home from school, and he had seemed very nice. Over the next several days, he would wait for her in the afternoon and walk with her, asking her questions about her favorite subjects and what type of music she liked. Fang said, "For the first time in my life, I felt like someone thought I was special. And for the first time in my life, someone told me I was beautiful." Those were the fateful words which led Fang to agree to go with the man one day, when he said he wanted to take her to the store to buy her something as special as she was. Instead, he took her to an unknown location where he hurt her greatly. Fang said that when he had finally left her alone one day, she escaped and somehow found her way back to the orphanage. But something inside of her heart had died during those two weeks, and she was not the same person she was before. She fell even deeper into despair when a few weeks later it was discovered that she was pregnant, and she had to go through an immediate abortion. Soon after, Fang disappeared again, and this time none of us ever heard where she had gone. I think of her with such sadness, and her words haunt me to this day: *"For the first time in my life, someone told me I was beautiful."* Just a few words from a stranger, but words which many orphaned children rarely if ever hear.

In 2015, Love Without Boundaries held our very first "Life Skills" camp for orphaned teens and young adults, bringing campers to Beijing from six Chinese provinces. The main purpose of the camp was to help these kids learn some crucial life information they would need when they went out on their own, such as personal budgeting, online safety, and sex education. One of the sessions was on self-esteem, and we quickly came to realize that it was the most impactful class of the week. The theme of the camp was, "The World is Better With Me In It," and many of the teens told us that no one had ever said that to them before. I am anxious to see these camps continue so that we can let even more great kids know that their lives do have enormous worth, even though I know it's impossible to reach every orphaned teen who needs to hear it. That never should stop us from trying, though.

A few years ago, I was on a trip when the man next to me on the plane asked me what I did for a living. I started to explain to him about our work in China and how many children around the world live as orphans. He got quiet for a moment and then said, "I bet there are days that you wish you didn't know that. It would probably be a whole lot easier on your heart."

Now it was my turn to be quiet. I thought about his words and about all the children and teens we have tried to help over the years. I thought about the sadness and grief that comes with working with people who are hurting, and I thought about the always present feeling that we are never doing enough; that there are always more kids in need than resources available. I quickly let his question run through my mind. Would it be better if I had never waded into these waters? Would it be better to be blissfully unaware of the realities that so many children around the world live in?

But the reality is I do know. And once you KNOW – once you have stepped into an orphanage and held the hands of kids who are searching for just one person to truly believe in them – there is no turning back. I carry the images of thousands of children in my heart, kids who have had every odd stacked against them. And yet, because of caring people in China and around the world who stepped forward to get involved, so many of them have been given a second chance at a happier life. Kids like Lin and Ming, now successful young adults, who never would have had the lives they do today without people believing in them.

I turned back to the man on my flight and told him that I supposed a lot of people would think he was right. Perhaps being completely unaware would somehow be "easier." But working with these children, who fight with everything they have, has changed me forever, and I believe they have changed me for the GOOD. They have shown me that nothing in our life should be taken for granted. Every day we are given a choice to either be a bystander or an active participant in this complex thing called life. While it is true that getting involved with children in need often means your heart will be broken, it also means your heart will be transformed. When you dare to reach out and take the hand of someone who is hurting, you allow the glimmer of hope that a miracle will grow. And when it does, nothing is more spectacular and humbling at the exact same time.

The Heart of an Orphan

Eighteen

Heroes

I'm sure most of us have had that classic school assignment where you have to write about your hero, and you're trying to figure out in 5th or 6th grade who exactly it is that inspires you. For some this is easy, and a person comes immediately to mind. Others have to go home and ask their parents for ideas. I'm sure for my older brother who loved golf, for example, someone like Arnold Palmer was a no-brainer for him. For me it was Jane Goodall, as, to a 10-year-old living in suburban Ohio, the thought of a young woman heading to Africa to study great apes was about the most daring thing I could imagine at the time.

As my own children have come home from school with this exact same assignment, I have thought more and more about what it really means to deserve the title of HERO. For me now, in my fifth decade of life, the faces which pop immediately into my mind are the children I have had the honor to work with. So many of them have faced such adversity and overcome such incredible odds, and yet they still manage to believe that each day can be a better one. They have taught me more about determination and the strength of the human spirit than any adult I have ever known. They will most likely never grace the front cover of magazines or be hailed as public heroes like many celebrity athletes and entertainers, but that is truly what they are: quiet heroes. Or as a recent adoption t-shirt summed up beautifully: "Braver than most."

I will never forget being in central China one bitterly cold winter and visiting a rural orphanage with conditions far poorer than most I had seen at the time. The orphanage was a single story row house-type facility, with metal bars over the doors and windows and extremely cold temperatures on the inside. As I walked into the main room, I saw rusty cribs filled with babies flat on their backs and then dozens of splintered chairs with wooden trays on them, each holding a child in a worn coat and split pants, and each with a bucket underneath serving as individual chamber pots. I could see that the kids were immobile due to the close fitting wooden trays, and they eyed me with understandable wariness as I came into the room. This orphanage was new to foreigners, only having just started international adoptions, and I knew many of the kids hadn't seen a lot of strangers like me before. I knelt down next to a boy with obvious dwarfism, who was so underweight that he could hardly hold his head upright. He looked at me with solemn eyes but didn't pull his hand away as I held onto his chapped, cold fingers. I glanced behind his chair and saw that the tiny baby in the crib behind him had blood coming from her ears, and I sadly realized that she must have had such a terrible untreated ear infection that her eardrums had ruptured. She was lying silently, staring up at the ceiling.

It is always such a complex situation when you visit an impoverished orphanage for the first time as you have no easy way of knowing whether the sad conditions are due to a lack of funding, or a lack of education in proper childcare, or, the worst of all, a lack of concern. If the ultimate hope is that you can form a friendship or partnership with the orphanage in order to work together with them to improve conditions for the kids, then that first visit is always an important one so that each side can gauge whether or not trust can be established. Breaking down into emotional tears or getting visibly upset about what you're seeing isn't a good way to build an enduring relationship, but, at the same time, I have had many moments where I have had to remind myself to keep smiling even while my heart was breaking. This was one of those days.

The next child I knelt down to talk with had the classic signs of a full blown scabies infestation, caused when tiny mites burrow into the upper layer of the skin to lay eggs. Scabies are very prevalent in crowded living conditions such as orphanages, and I could clearly see the red burrowing lines on his arms and across his forehead where the female mites had tunneled under his skin. The little boy was far too pale, a classic sign of anemia, but he cocked his head to the side to study me. When I reached over to warm his hands in mine, he gave me a glorious smile full of decaying teeth. I cemented our new friendship when I pulled out a baggie full of Kix cereal for him to eat, and that definitely got the sudden and immediate attention of all the other kids sitting in their wooden chairs as well.

I glanced over and saw a little boy very somberly studying me. He looked to be about eight or nine, and he had the most beautiful face and the kind of eyes where you can look at them and see the deep intelligence inside. He was in a low-seated wooden chair that was clearly too small for his body. The orphanage director came over to tell me that his name was Jiang and that he had been born with cerebral palsy, a neurological condition which impacts muscle movement. I feel CP is probably one of the most misunderstood medical conditions around the world as a majority of people think that CP and severe intellectual disabilities automatically go hand-in-hand, which isn't the case. While some forms of CP can cause cognitive issues, just as many kids with this special need have completely normal intelligence. They just have bodies which don't always move the way they wish. We have done our very best at LWB to help educate as many orphanage workers as possible that kids with CP deserve the same opportunities as every other child, but it has been an uphill battle at times. Even today, many orphaned children with files that state a CP diagnosis also have "mental retardation" checked automatically by rural doctors as well.

When I first met Jiang that day, he had an aura of weariness enveloping him as if he just knew that sitting in that splintered chair was all his life was ever going to be. As I started talking to him, it was clear after just a few moments what a beautiful and gentle soul was trapped inside. His nanny told me that he couldn't walk easily and so it was simpler for him just to sit all day. Every day. I left the orphanage later that afternoon with Jiang's face stored deeply in my heart, wondering what we could possibly do to make his life a little brighter.

Thankfully, an answer presented itself soon after. We learned that his city had a local physical therapy center, where families could send their children who had issues such as CP, for daily therapy and exercise. We, of course, asked immediately if Jiang could be accepted into the program if LWB paid the fees, and they agreed to take him on a short-term basis. The next time I visited his town, I was able to see him at the PT center, and he greeted me with an enormous smile. He showed me all the artwork he had been working on, and it was clear that he had a special gift with drawing. He also treated me to several songs he had been learning, and the physical therapists got him up so he could show me how he was strengthening his muscles in order to walk a bit further each day. I knew the PT center time was just temporary for Jiang, but I left that day with a much lighter feeling in my heart, happy that he was able to have this opportunity to work with nurses and therapists to improve his muscle tone.

When it was time for Jiang to graduate from the PT program, we knew he needed more individualized care than the orphanage could provide; so we arranged for him to go into our foster care program. Since none of the public schools near him at that time would accept a child with his degree of muscle impairment, we also arranged for a local teacher to visit him in foster care a few times a week to tutor him in reading and math and to work with him on art projects. I knew it was far from ideal for a child who was so bright and eager to learn, but it was honestly the best we could arrange at that time. We helped purchase a walker for Jiang as well so that he could continue working his leg muscles each day, even though his foster home was extremely rural with dirt roads which weren't very conducive to wheelchairs or adaptive equipment. Most of all, however, we continued to tell anyone who would listen that this young boy was special and that he deserved a chance at adoption. At that time, it was still very rare for an orphanage to agree to prepare the adoption paperwork for kids with more severe special needs. Some local officials didn't want to lose face over such a child representing their city in the U.S. or Europe, but they also couldn't comprehend that families would purposely choose an older child who couldn't walk or who hadn't been educated.

By this time, we had built an incredibly strong relationship with Jiang's orphanage. We had done over 50 surgeries for them and had established one of our largest foster care programs there, and so they finally agreed to file his adoption paperwork after realizing we were never going to stop asking for it to be done. I had assured them continually that I was positive a family could be found, while also knowing inside that he had three very serious strikes against him ever finding a permanent home: First, he was a boy; second, he was older; and third, he had a special need which instantly caused many people to think, "We could never take that on." So while I was assuring the orphanage that lots of families would love a son like Jiang, I was also praying nightly that God would plant the seed in a family's heart that he was supposed to be their son.

As soon as his paperwork made it to the national level, we began advocating for him in our newsletter and on our blog, but no one stepped forward for him. Jiang was now 12 years old, and I knew that his time was running out to find a permanent family. We all felt a sense of urgency to make his case widely known. I visited Jiang in China during this time, and he asked me why no one had chosen him yet. How do you even answer that question? What do you say to a child who is looking at you with such sincere hope? He told me quietly, "I would be so kind to a mom and dad if they chose me," and I knew to my core that he was speaking a real truth.

At the time, Jiang was living in foster care with a four-year-old boy who also had mobility issues due to being born with a malformation of his feet and legs. They were wonderful foster brothers, and little Wei absolutely adored his older brother Jiang, wanting to be at his side at all times. They were inseparable, and, in one of my favorite photos of them, they have their arms tightly around each other in a wonderful cheek-to-cheek hug. When I learned that Wei had been chosen by a family for adoption, I knew it was going to be incredibly hard on Jiang's heart to say goodbye to him. I also realized that, once again, another child would be meeting his forever family while Jiang remained behind. The unfairness of it all was overwhelming to me, but we continued to advocate and asked everyone we knew to spread the word that Jiang was still waiting for a family to bring him home as well.

In January of 2011, we ran another story about Jiang as many wonderful people had donated towards an ever-increasing adoption grant for him. It included a photo of Jiang standing proudly with his walker, with one hand protectively on his little brother's shoulder. In the blog, we talked about how much they loved each other and how much Jiang wanted a family of his own. Seven thousand miles away from China, a woman named Amy read those words, and God began working on her family's heart in a very special way. You see, Amy and her husband were the ones already in the process to adopt four-year-old Wei, and now they began praying about whether Jiang was supposed to join their family as well. Who doesn't love a happy ending? I was overjoyed to soon receive an email from Amy that Jiang and Wei were going to go from being LWB foster siblings to legally adopted brothers as her family was filing the paperwork to bring them both home at the same time. They knew that there wasn't going to be anything "easy" about going through not only a double adoption but an older child adoption as well. They knew that Jiang was going to be almost 13 when they brought him home and that he had never participated in a real school. They knew there were enormous unknowns in his medical file and that there were huge challenges in even physically navigating China with a child who was unable to walk more than a few steps on his own. They had faith, however, that they were going to be able to make it all come together so that the boys would remain forever as brothers.

I feel very blessed to still be in contact with Jiang and his mom now that he has been home in America for many years. He actually now volunteers for LWB, which I admit makes me have a huge lump in my throat when I think about it as he has gone from a young child needing our assistance all those years ago to now a wonderful young man wanting to help those who remain in orphanage care. He is one of my heroes, and he inspires me to keep going and to never give up, even when things seem impossible. His story deserves to be told as more people need to understand that there are millions of children around the world who are living without encouragement, just as he was. Kids who wake up every single day devoid of hope. If more people would take the time to really listen with their hearts, how many more children could be impacted? I have told you my story of when I met this remarkable young man, but now I want you to hear it in his very own words because I want him to be one of your heroes as well.

Jiang's story

In 1997, I was born with cerebral palsy in Henan, China. I was the second child of my birth parents, who owned a little shop where they sold snacks and toys. I lived with my birth parents until I was around eight years old. My memories of my early years include spending most of my time sitting in my parents' shop while they were busy running it. I sat in a little wooden chair behind the counter and when I needed to go somewhere, my father had to carry me there since I wasn't able to walk. As I got older and heavier, my father complained to my mother that I was getting too difficult to care for. He and my mother had fights about what should be done with me.

One day, a car pulled up to our shop and two men got out. They spoke with my father and then picked me up and put me in the car. My father gave the men boxes of cigarettes and told me to be good and do what the men said. There were tears in his eyes as he said goodbye to me. The car pulled away from our shop and that was the last time I saw my father or any of my birth family. The two men drove me to an orphanage in a nearby city and left me there. I remember crying when the nannies told me this was my new home.

My life at the orphanage was the same day in and day out, unless we had visitors. At night, I slept in a metal crib that was too small for me since I was around eight years old. The crib bottom was covered in a rough mat which smelled badly. In the morning, the ayis would get me and the other children out of our cribs and place us into wooden chairs with trays made of a flat board. There was no way for me to get out of the chair and children who were more mobile were tied with ropes around their waist to keep them from climbing out of their chairs. Each chair had a round hole in the seat and metal bowls were placed under each seat for when we used the bathroom. Flies swarmed around the bowls and our chairs and the smell was terrible. We had our meals in the chairs and we stayed in the chairs all day with nothing to play with or do. My entertainment was watching the flies crawling on my chair. After dinner, we were put back in our cribs for the night. When visitors came, which was a rare occurrence, we were put in better clothing and were sometimes given toys to play with. That was my life for around a year or two.

In 2006, Amy Eldridge came to visit my orphanage. She saw the conditions us children were living in and wanted to do something to help. Love Without Boundaries teamed up with the orphanage to improve our lives. I was placed with several different foster families over the next five years. Love Without Boundaries provided me with a walker so I could get around more independently and I also received physical therapy. Foster care wasn't perfect but I was much happier in all my foster homes than I had been at the orphanage. In the foster homes things were cleaner and didn't smell bad. The food in my foster homes was much better quality too and was served warm instead of cold. I wasn't hungry anymore like I had been in the orphanage. When I lived with my foster families, I had things to do so life was no longer boring. I learned how to draw and paint, I was given chores to do, I played outside and visited with neighbors. Love Without Boundaries provided a tutor for some of the foster children including me. I enjoyed attending classes with the other kids, making friends, and learning how to read, write, do basic math, and sing Chinese songs.

I had a foster sister who was close to my age who I lived with for a couple years. When I found out she was being adopted, I felt like I was being left behind and I wished for a family to adopt me as well. Amy Eldridge visited me in my foster home at this time and I asked her why no one wanted to adopt me. After my foster sister was adopted, I got a new little foster brother, Wei, who was almost four years old. When I found out that both of us were going to be adopted by the same family in America, I was very excited.

The time eventually came for us to meet our new adoptive family. I was nervous but also very happy to finally be getting a family. My adoptive family already had a son and daughter who were both younger than me but older than Wei. My new sister had been adopted from China four years before Wei and me. She had also been sponsored by Love Without Boundaries which is how my family found out about Wei and me needing a family.

Adjusting to a new family was hard at first because everything was new and I didn't speak English. I had to go to many doctors and that scared me since I didn't know what they would do to me. I learned English pretty quickly and I also learned that doctors in America are kind and gentle. I have gotten to do so many fun things since coming to America that I never would have been able to do if I stayed an orphan in China. My favorite places to go now are shopping, the movies, book stores, museums, aquariums, and other trips. My mom home schools me and I really like reading, spelling, writing, history, and science. I also get to go to church and I learned that Jesus loves me and will always be with me. The best thing about being adopted is finally having a family that loves me and who will always be my family. I have a mom, dad, brothers, sisters, grandparents, aunts, uncles, and cousins who care about me and love me. My wish is that more families in America will adopt kids in China and give them a new life and a family to love them.

When I first read Jiang's own words, the line which pierced my heart the most was, "My entertainment was the flies crawling on my chair." For anyone reading this book, I want you to let those words sink deeply into your heart. This is the reality for far too many children who have been abandoned with medical needs. These are not nameless, faceless orphans. These are living, breathing individuals, and their situations are far too real. Every child currently living in institutional care has a story of loss and a need for someone to believe that his or her life matters. We all need to take the time to really listen, and we can't turn away and pretend they aren't there, because THEY ARE. The way we respond to the most vulnerable of our world speaks volumes about who we really are inside. Years ago, I knelt down to a little boy in a splintered, wooden chair who spoke to me with his eyes about who he really was, and his life motivated me to try and do more. That is the very definition of a hero, isn't it – someone who inspires us to be better than we currently are. All around the world, orphanages are filled with children just like Jiang, desperately hoping for someone to see the beauty inside them. While I know that adoption isn't for every family, we all have the ability to keep spreading the word about how many children are still waiting to come HOME.

Nineteen

Us Versus Them

To say I have seen great changes in China's economy since I first traveled there in 2000 is a massive understatement. Every time I go back now, the major cities are filled with more sports cars; more neon signs advertising Gucci, Prada, and Cartier; and a growing trend of conspicuous consumption. Construction is everywhere you look, as entire farming villages are disappearing forever, making way for high-rise government apartment complexes and large shopping malls. Housing prices in many regions have skyrocketed, and affluent Chinese citizens now travel the world on luxurious vacations. As China's meteoric economic rise began being covered almost daily on cable news stations, I began being asked more and more why China deserved any financial help from charitable organizations now. This is a very understandable question, especially since so much of our media coverage on China is geared to make us fear the country as a whole, with "China Rising" in big red letters often flashing behind the news anchor.

One morning I had a phone call from someone who had read an article about LWB helping children overseas. What I initially thought was going to be a pleasant call actually gave me great pause when the woman asked sharply, "But why should WE help THEM?" There it was – us versus them – and I knew she was asking why Americans should help the Chinese, since at the government level the two countries seem to be constantly engaged in power struggles now. But as someone doing humanitarian work, with children who are often caught in literal life and death struggles, what I also heard her asking was this: Why should individuals in the U.S. ever help anyone living outside our borders? The caller's use of the word "them" cut through my heart like a knife, as I know very well that the "them" she had bitterly mouthed are in reality tiny babies left in cardboard boxes and toddlers in shock at suddenly finding themselves abandoned by their parents. "THEM" are actual children who are struggling to breathe with heart disease and who are often hungry and malnourished. As she continued to try to shove home her point on why what I was doing was somehow "wrong" and actually un-American, I closed my eyes and gave thanks that I get to work each day with hundreds of volunteers who understand that there are no politics involved when a child is hurting.

I used to want to make a video to illustrate this point better, but I was never able to actually pull it together. I wanted it to open with a woman in the U.S. getting ready to leave her house in the morning and stepping out to find a newborn baby on her doorstep in urgent need of medical help. What would anyone do in that moment? We'd grab our phone and call 9-1-1 and move heaven and earth to make sure that baby's life was saved. We'd open our wallets if it meant sparing his life, and we'd probably go to the hospital and keep checking to make sure the baby was okay, since he was left right on our front porch after all.

Then I wanted to cut to a scene of the same woman on vacation hundreds of miles from her home, let's say in Canada. She's out hiking one day in the woods, where she suddenly comes across the same abandoned baby under a tree, obviously in need of medical help. Does she turn away from the baby since he's not from her own hometown? Does she keep walking past since he was born north of the New York state line? Of course not; that would be ludicrous to imagine. She'd do the exact same thing as if the baby was on her front porch. She'd move heaven and earth to get him to a hospital and make sure the little boy's life is saved.

For the final scene, it would be a birth mother in China or Uganda or Haiti abandoning the same baby, knowing she can't provide the child with the medical care needed. Is that innocent baby suddenly unworthy of care for being born outside the U.S.? Is a baby in an orphanage overseas any less deserving of compassion and our immediate help? Of course they aren't. When we learn of children anywhere in the world who are sick and frightened and far too alone, we should try and help them as if they were right in front of us on our own porch steps. Does the simple fact that they are a few thousand miles away make their needs any less critical or important?

All across the world, there are incredible efforts underway by governments to lift their citizens out of poverty, but, as we know from the needs here in our own country, eliminating all hunger, disease, and barriers to good education is essentially impossible. There will always be poverty, and there will always be people living with sorrow we don't even want to imagine. That means there will also always be an opportunity for each of us to try and make the world a more beautiful and compassionate place, both in our own backyards and around the globe. Absolutely China's economic growth has been staggering, but that doesn't change the fact that over 80 million people there still live on less than $2 a day. Their economic growth doesn't change the fact that their birth defect rate has been skyrocketing, leaving countless children in need of medical care which their impoverished families are unable to provide. Their financial rise hasn't slowed the abandonment of children either, with almost a million kids living as orphans, and far too many not having their most basic needs met. All over the world, even in the wealthiest of countries, there will always be children who fall through the cracks of the system, and so there will always be a place for charities to reach out a hand to try and pull them back up. How grateful I am that there are organizations around the globe that are trying to stand in the gap for kids in crisis right this moment, and I give thanks every day that God led my heart to China. How I wish there was a way for anyone who divides humanity into "us versus them" to spend time with the local people they feel are so undeserving of help. People like Han, who I first met as part of one of our cleft surgery exchanges. No one could meet this remarkable young lady and not be moved by all she has overcome.

Han was born with a really wide bilateral cleft lip, and her birth parents had abandoned her as a baby in a rural field shortly after she came into the world. Thankfully, a man passing by that day found her bundled up near the dusty road, and, when he saw the tiny baby had been left all on her own, he gently picked her up and took her home to his wife. The couple decided to keep the little girl and raise her as their own despite the fact that they were extremely poor. In fact, I learned that the father made just 10 rmb per week (about $1.20 at that time), making local deliveries on his rusty bicycle.

This couple adored little Han, despite the local villagers saying she was cursed and someone to be publicly shunned. Han's new parents raised her with kindness and lots of love, but they were never able to afford for her to have the life-changing cleft lip surgery she needed. She lived her entire childhood feeling like an outsider in her community, staying indoors and pouring her heart into studying and reading books in the safety of her small home, but dreaming that someday she could face the outside world with a normal appearance.

When Han was 19 years old, she and her father came to one of our cleft trips, traveling many hours with the hope that she might finally receive the healing she needed. Her father very quietly asked our team if she was now too old to have cleft surgery, and Han told us shyly that she knew it was probably impossible for her to be included on our busy schedule. Of course, we made room and performed her operation, and the entire team was deeply moved by her tender spirit. Following her surgery, she sent us the letter below:

I am almost completely recovered now. I believe that it will not be long to see a true me living freely like other ordinary girls. These are my dreams for so many years. Thinking about possibilities and a future life, I am very happy and grateful from the bottom of my heart because I know all these changes were given to me by warm hearted people. I still don't know who are my own biological parents; it's my adopted parents, who picked me up from the road when I was abandoned, that gave me a new life. They are very poor but I can feel their love. Recollecting the old times, I got used to harsh ridiculous remarks, cold eyes, and snobbish comments from ignorant bystanders. Weeping and sleeplessness in dark nights are still vivid in my memories. Life, year after year, has taught me a lot and made me stronger and now more optimistic. In the past, even though I had never said anything about a cleft operation to my current adopted parents, I knew that they were anxious but all helpless, without the ability to help me. I could only accept this as my fate. I am like other girls who love to have sweet and beautiful dreams. Just before I went to see your team, I dreamed that I would meet good-hearted people someday. This miracle appeared unexpectedly and came to me in an unbelievably fast way. To tell the truth, it was nothing more than trying my luck when I went to your team. My past living experience taught me not to expect miracles; that they only appear in storybooks. But everything went smoothly. Thinking about all these now, I still feel that I myself was in the dream of fantasy. The pain and burden in my heart has disappeared; only a happy smile is left.

For 19 years, Han had lived believing that there would never be a real future for herself. For 19 years, people had shunned her as one who was completely unworthy. And yet, because kind people were able to see beyond boundaries and give from their hearts, Han's life was changed forever. She and I went on to become friends, and I was honored to meet her entire family on one of my trips back to her home province. I will never forget the tears of gratitude from her father, who clung tightly to my hand and thanked us for helping his beloved daughter. He and I were the exact same age at the time, both in our 40s, but he looked like an old man, stooped over with arthritis from hard manual labor and working their meager field. His face was deeply lined with wrinkles of worry, and you could just see the difficult hardships he had lived through trying to provide for his family on just pennies a day.

We all knew from the first time we met Han that she was extremely intelligent, and all of those years of quietly studying inside had given her a brilliant mind. We encouraged her to sit for the grueling "gaokao" college entrance examination in China, a multi-day exam which is given just once per year. The gaokao is often called the most pressure-packed test in the world, but we knew that Han was incredibly smart and had confidence she would pass. She finally agreed to register for the exam, even while telling us that, since her dad made less than $10 a month, it would be impossible for her to ever attend college. We told her to humor us and take the exam anyway, and Han soon got a formal letter saying she had been admitted to a university in far western China to study accounting and business. Thanks to some amazing education sponsors, we were able to tell Han to pack her bags. With both extreme excitement for a new adventure but also real anxiety about leaving her small home for the first time in her life, Han boarded a train on her own. I'm thrilled to say that she quickly became the top student in her class, and, in fact, she didn't even need our financial assistance after the first year because the university awarded her multiple academic scholarships. Her dad was so incredibly proud of his daughter, telling me through his tears that he couldn't believe his family's cycle of poverty was being changed because his daughter was going to become the first college graduate in his family's history.

Was Han a THEM? Was her gentle father, who had mercifully picked up a tiny abandoned baby, a THEM? I don't understand how people can live with that sort of division in their hearts. I think that anyone who lives in an "us versus them" world is missing out on one of the true wonders of the human experience. I still can't believe that I get to meet people all around the world because of my job. My life has been enriched in countless ways because I get to keep learning every day about cultures and customs all over this amazing, incredible earth. When I think that supporters in Spain or Australia can all come together through LWB to help a tiny baby in Asia receive surgery or to help a little boy who can't walk get his very first wheelchair... well, that is just miraculous to me. The Internet has made our world so very small, and it has brought us together in astonishing ways to share gestures of compassion with those who need our help the most.

Despite the dazzling lights and high rises in Beijing and Shanghai, the poverty I have seen traveling through the rural countryside of China is still immense. I have gone into the western mountains on winding dirt roads coming upon villages which are like stepping back in time 100 years. I meet kids who sleep on the ground, whose bodies are stunted from poor nutrition. Kids whose only source of heat in the winter is a tiny coal stove and who have to walk miles on often dangerous dirt roads and wooden bridges just to have a chance at education. Kids whose homes don't have bathrooms and who look suntanned until you realize it is just dirt and grime worked into their skin as their family can only afford to go to the public showers once a year to bathe. And yet the hospitality I am shown when I visit these regions humbles me to the core. At almost every home I enter, tea is immediately made. I am offered fruit or rice, and I'm allowed to hear their somber stories of World War II occupation or the chaos of the Cultural Revolution. For so many, it is a very difficult life story they share.

One of my favorite regions to visit in China is the southwestern province of Guizhou. This region is still one of China's poorest economically, but I feel one of the richest when it comes to natural beauty and diversity of culture. Guizhou is a land of tall mountains and terraced rice fields, home to many of China's ethnic minority groups, such as the Miao, Yi, and Dong peoples. We have been helping orphaned children in Guizhou since 2005, and we have done many projects for extremely rural villages which are home to many of China's "Left Behind" kids. More than 60 million children in China are growing up without the care of their parents, left behind when their moms and dads head to the larger cities in the east hoping to find work. Many of these impoverished children are being raised by elderly and often ill grandparents, while others must fend for themselves completely. To put that into perspective, 60 million is the entire population of Italy or the U.K. It is also just slightly smaller than the entire population of all children in the U.S., and yet in China that many kids are growing up right now without parents by their side.

On one of my trips to Guizhou, our final day happened to coincide with the annual Miao dragon boat races, one of the largest local festivals held each year. Over 20 different villages come together for this special day, each arriving in their own unique traditional dress; so, of course, we wanted to go. Right as we arrived to the town where the festival was being held, we noticed a little boy walking slowly up a dirt road with his great grandmother. She was bent completely over at her waist and looked extremely frail. I had seen so many people in this region who were permanently stooped over at an almost 90 degree angle, and I learned that it was from working the rice fields their entire lives.

The little boy had stopped to talk to his grandma, and it was clear that they had come a very long way and were trying to figure out how to make it the remaining mile to the village. There was a large bundle in the dirt road next to them, and it seemed like the little boy was struggling to know whether to carry their possessions or help his obviously tired and weak grandma walk on the bumpy road.

We approached them to see if we could help in any way, and the little boy looked up at us and suddenly burst into tears. His entire face was filled with such despair that my heart immediately fell. The grandmother then looked up, and suddenly she began to cry as well. She reached out to grab my hand while speaking to us in the Miao language, which none of us could understand. We didn't need to grasp her words, though, as it was clear they were filled with complete sorrow.

The little boy told us through his sobs that his father had left home many months ago to find work. They had recently gotten the message that he had died somewhere in the east, but no one had told them how or what had become of him after his death. His mother had also gone east to find work, and so he was left behind in his rural village to care for his grandmothers. On the day we met him, he was trying to get his great grandmother from his tiny mountain village almost ten miles away to his aunt's house in the larger river town. I think the burden of responsibility on his ten-year-old shoulders was just too much for him to bear that day. When we had asked if he was okay, he finally broke down.

We picked up the cloth sack he had been carrying, which weighed at least 30 pounds, and then slowly made our way to the center of town, holding tightly to the grandmother's arm to give her support. The entire way she continued to cry.

After we finally got the grandmother settled, we asked the little boy, Li, if he would like to be our guide that day at the festival. He quickly agreed and proceeded to tell us the history of the dragon boat races and the significance of every ceremony performed. He was such a smart little boy and obviously very proud of his Miao heritage. While we were waiting for the dragon races to start, our Chinese director Cindy took Li to the nearby street market to get him some food. When they came back, he was so excited to show us that she had bought him a fishing pole as well. He told us he would be able to catch lots of fish now for his grandmas to help with their meals. I told her I would love to buy him a toy, but Cindy explained that he was now the man of the home with the death of his father, and toys would be an insult. He had chosen the fishing pole to provide for his family, and my heart was heavy to think about the responsibility he knew he had to shoulder at just age ten.

Cindy had written her cell phone number on a piece of paper for him, telling him he could call her if he ever needed anything. He was sitting right in front of me on the river bank, and I watched him take out that piece of paper a hundred times during that afternoon. At one point, I heard him slowly saying the numbers to himself over and over again. I realized he was committing Cindy's number to his memory in case he ever lost the tiny scrap of paper. I tapped Cindy on the shoulder to show him what he was doing, and both of us got tears in our eyes as we watched him trying his best to memorize the phone number which could bring him help in an emergency.

Soon the sun started to go down on the horizon, and we asked the little boy how he would get home. He told us he would walk back up the mountain by himself, but we, of course, insisted on taking him in the van. As we drove the many miles up the winding roads to his village, I kept thinking of him making that journey every time he needed to go into town. When the road ended, we climbed up a steep path and stairway to finally reach his wooden home, overlooking a winding river.

As the little boy talked more about his mom being gone and learning of his father's death, he began to cry again. He was trying his very best to control his weeping, and it was obvious he felt caught between being a scared little boy needing reassurance while having to be brave as the man of the home now. His loneliness was so raw that it honestly hurt to look in his eyes. He finally was able to control his tears, and very reluctantly we knew it was time to say goodbye.

Our driver told us it wouldn't be safe to be on the mountainous dirt roads in the complete dark; so all we could do at that point was to get the address of his village (which we have since learned does not have mail service). It was very sobering to say goodbye to him, wondering what the future held for this intelligent, kind, and responsible little boy. Would he somehow get a higher education, or would he stop after middle school to work the fields? Would the deep sorrow and longing for his parents we so clearly saw on his face somehow be able to be eased? I knew there had been several child suicides in this province recently, "Left Behind" kids who had chosen to take their own lives when the hardships of being on their own became too much for them to bear. In one tragic case, four siblings – a boy and three girls, aged five to 14 – were found dead at their home in a rural village. They had poisoned themselves after their parents had abandoned them to find work elsewhere, leaving a suicide note from the older brother which read, "I'm 14 now. I dream about death, and yet that dream never comes true. Today it must finally come to pass." As we drove away from Li's tiny village, I thought again of how much we all need people in our lives to support and encourage us. It can be so very hard to do life when you feel completely alone.

I continue to hope that, with each passing year, we as adults realize that, regardless of where a child happens to be born, they are so deserving of love. I like to think that when we help children around the world, we are not only helping that child have a better life, but we are also spreading seeds of empathy and understanding to those surrounding them. When we chose the name of our charity, "Love Without Boundaries," we truly believed that love could bridge any barrier between countries. Indeed, love is the one thing that can unite us into a beautiful humanity. So until every child born is safe, warm, and fed, I continue to give thanks for those around the world who realize that we are one human race, and that this life is infinitely better when shared. Every baby around the world cries in the same language. We, as adults, should love in the same language as well.

Twenty

Unity and Abandonment

According to China's legal codes, child abandonment is a criminal offense, punishable by imprisonment of up to five years. In reality, though, these laws are rarely enforced, and so all around the country children are left each and every day by their families. Officials in China place the number of children being abandoned at upwards of 100,000 per year, and the government acknowledges that it is one of the biggest societal concerns China still faces today. I have sadly seen the fragile condition of far too many infants and babies who have been abandoned under the cover of darkness in such a wide variety of places. All of us can easily understand that a one-day-old infant isn't supposed to be left outside on a hillside, or behind a factory, or on a busy street. Babies are so defenseless, completely dependent on those around them. They, of course, can't survive without an adult to watch over them, and the consequences can be tragic when help doesn't come immediately. We had one beautiful little baby in our programs who was found by a wild animal before she was discovered by a passing stranger. The bottom half of her foot had to be amputated, and I remember the utter sadness which washed over me when I was told of her condition as she arrived at the orphanage. Occasionally, the stories of abandoned children make international news, such as the newborn baby with cleft from Guangxi Province, miraculously found after being buried alive in a box for ten days, or the little girl who was left inside a sewer pipe in a public toilet in Beijing. Local and worldwide outrage comes to the forefront of the news for a few days in those cases, and then their stories are soon forgotten. It is important to remember, though, that every single day hundreds of babies and children are left on their own, often with no trace of the parents to be found, and each and every one of them has a story just as important.

Because this is very emotional work, I admit that I usually try not to think very much about the abandonment part, instead just throwing myself into trying to figure out the next steps to get the child help. Do they need medical care? Or a specialized formula? Taking swift action always helps, but there have definitely been times in the past when we were called about a child and the circumstances of how they were found will make me feel such a myriad of emotions.

As an adoptive parent myself, I always try to be respectful of birth parents, and when I'm in orphanages I frequently talk about how adoptive families often try to honor their child's first parents. Many have ceremonies for special times like Mother's Day, perhaps releasing balloons with messages to a birth mom, or even setting an extra place at the table on holidays. Many of the nannies in orphanages I have spoken with really struggle with this idea; I think most likely because they have seen up close and personal the consequences of leaving a child outside in the elements. Many have told me those who abandon are "bad people," and I have tried my best to share my feelings that in a country where abortion is so readily and legally available, and where the practice of infanticide is a very real part of their ancient history, I know many adoptive parents believe that the fact that our children are still alive is something to be honored. I have been in several cities over the years in China where orphanage officials have pointed out a stream or a lake while telling me it has a name such as "River of Sorrows," known to be a location where in past generations unwanted babies would be drowned. Each time I am shown such a place, I give thanks that my own children were found safely.

The Chinese government recognizes that figuring out a way to protect the children being left is a serious matter which must be addressed. In 2013, the Ministry of Civil Affairs called for the creation of baby safe houses in many Chinese cities. These "baby hatches" were supposed to be a warm and safe refuge to ensure that children were immediately given care after being left. They were not without controversy, though, as some felt it was encouraging people to publicly break the very clear Chinese laws regarding child abandonment. Unfortunately, as news of the safe havens spread, many locations were completely overwhelmed by the number of children being dropped off. Several facilities had to close their doors completely, such as the safe house in Guangzhou which received 262 babies, all with serious health problems, in just 48 days. It was impossible for the local orphanage to keep up with such a tide of abandoned children. There are no easy answers to this national problem as parents struggle to cope with the ever-increasing number of babies born with birth defects. So are the parents who abandon their children "bad people," like many of the orphanage nannies have expressed to me?

Many years ago we were called by a rural orphanage about an emergency baby with cleft lip they had found on Christmas Eve in the blinding snow. She wasn't found until morning, and, by the time she was discovered, her ears and toes were severely frostbitten. We rushed her to the hospital right away, but doctors told us we were too late to save the frozen tissue; so the tops of her ears and seven of her toes had to be amputated. I think since it was Christmas, when I already was feeling overwhelmed by the typical stress of the holiday season, seeing the photos of the little girl put me over the edge. I was pacing around angrily when our hospital manager called to give me an update, and I remember saying something like, "I'm furious at her birth family. Who could leave a newborn outside in a snowstorm? Who sets a baby down on the ground in the freezing snow and simply walks away?" I thought that was a very valid question, and I expected our Chinese manager to join in my rage and say, "I know! How awful of them!" But then she said something that I still pull up to this day. She said, "You have to remember that we don't know anything about how she came to be there. Maybe the mother-in-law was threatening to end the child's life by putting her in a bucket of ash. Maybe the person who stole away with her in the night was actually trying to save her, hoping someone would discover the baby and take her somewhere safe. Maybe when it came down to the imminent death of the baby, versus even the smallest chance at life, the person who left her did so with desperate hope."

Yes, that silenced me immediately. She had just shown me a completely different scenario than I had originally envisioned, and I was imagining them side by side in my head. In one scene the birth parent is appalled by the baby's special need and callously leaves the newborn in the snow, not caring whether she lives or dies. And in the other, a panicked birth parent, knowing relatives will not allow such a child to live and bring shame to the family name, quickly sneaks out into the snowstorm and leaves the baby with a prayer that someone will find her and keep her safe. So which was it? I realized in that moment, yet again, that we simply don't know. None of us had been there the day the baby girl was left in the snowstorm, and so any judgment at all would be completely unfair. My anger fizzled out immediately, and then the question of how to best help her urgently replaced it instead.

There is no getting around the fact that child abandonment is a sorrowful thing. One of the things which became clear to all of us with LWB as we helped more and more children needing medical care was that those of us working with orphaned children also needed to ask ourselves what more we could be doing to stop orphans from being created in the first place. Over the years, we had met so many impoverished families in crisis. As word spread in hospitals that we were helping children who were orphaned get free medical care, we began having rural families beg us to take their children from them if it meant they could somehow be healed. Time and again, we were approached by families who were willing to relinquish the children they loved to our care if it meant their lives would be saved. How many of us have had to ever consider the enormity of that sacrifice? No parent should ever feel that level of pure desperation, and so I was thrilled when we created a new program in 2008 called the Unity Initiative, with the sincere goal of family preservation. It has been one of the most rewarding projects I have ever worked on. We have been blessed to meet so many wonderful and loving families, who just happen to live in crushing poverty. Families like baby Lang's, whose mom and dad were rural migrant workers and who loved their little boy fiercely. His father wrote the following letter to us, asking for help:

In December, my son Lang came to this world. I was so happy. I named him "Langlang" with the hope that he would be joyful and extroverted, and with dreams he will have a smooth life. I thought life would be happy from then on, but Langlang was found to have severe heart disease when he was three months old. Doctors in our region told me only the big hospitals in Beijing, Shanghai, and Guangzhou could fix it, but that it would cost a lot of money. I am a tough person but I could not help crying.

We tried all means to ask for help. We borrowed money from relatives and friends. We finally knew that we would never be able to raise all the funds needed. But we went to Shanghai, and the diagnosis was still complicated heart disease. The doctor said his surgery would be 80,000 rmb! Many told us we could give him up, and we even thought of it. But each time when I put him on the bed, Langlang would cling to my clothing tightly. He is such a good boy.

Langlang is only six months old. He is so smart and has brought us so much joy. But he is getting more and more sick. He turns blue all the time. He is very weak.

Life should be respected. We do not have the right to give up on his life. We brought him to this world, and we should give him the right to live. But reality is cruel. We have tried hard to raise money but do not have enough.

We are migrant workers with limited ability. We feel so helpless and know how precious life is. But we do not know how to make it through. We have tried our best to raise money and will keep trying. We hope to get your help. Though we have never met, we appreciate your help to save the life of Langlang and bring hope to us.

Of course we said we would help them. I was so happy we could be there for Langlang's family and provide the remaining funds required for the heart surgery he so desperately needed. We were thrilled when he recovered beautifully from his operation and could be carried proudly back home to his village, now a wonderful and healthy pink color. A few months after his operation, Lang's father wrote us again:

Dear all LWB friends,

This is the father of Lang, the heart baby. On behalf of my son and all the other family members, I sincerely express our appreciation for all you did for us.

Earlier this year, it was determined that Lang suffers from Complex Heart Disease by the People's Hospital in our province. Confronted by such bad news, all our family collapsed like a dam bursting. I even did not know how we could go on. It was you, LWB, giving your hand to our family in our most helpless period of time. It was you, my dearest LWB, who saved my son's life. In our saddest and most helpless days, it was you who helped us contact the surgeons in Shanghai and arrange everything for us. It was you who funded us when we had no way to borrow more money to afford the huge treatment fees, and it was you gave us psychological consideration and support.

Once we arrived in Shanghai, a city that was once a friendless place for us, it was LWB Manager Wang who gave us a relative's warm concern and guided us when we felt absent-minded. He taught us how to go by bus or metro and arranged all hospitalization procedures by himself. He was so considerate, and some other patients in the sickroom misunderstood that Manager Wang was the grandfather of Lang because of his concern. It was such a moving thing for us.

We must be thankful for small mercies. Your love has crossed oceans and boundaries! It is such a pity that we cannot say thanks to you face to face. But we will store all these up in our heart. As Lang grows up, we will teach him how to be a good man and how to be grateful, in order to acknowledge your good deeds to save his life.

Yep, that left me in a puddle of tears, but these are the types of letters we receive from parents frantically trying to find help for their children. It is sobering to think that often it is just a few thousand dollars which can make the difference between them tragically abandoning their child in desperation or keeping them united as a family.

Anyone who is a parent knows the terrible feelings experienced when your child becomes sick. As a mom to seven, I, of course, have had many times where I have had that panicked feeling in my heart when one of them became seriously ill. One of the worst times for me was when my son Patrick suffered a severe head injury, with two areas of intense bleeding in his brain. I remember feeling like I couldn't take a complete breath, and my heart didn't seem to be able to fully beat as I waited for news on whether doctors felt they could help him. And yet I knew inside that we were fortunate to have medical insurance, and that the doctors at Vanderbilt were going to do everything needed in order to save his life, regardless of whether or not I had enough money to pay them. I compare that now to the families who ask for us help through our Unity Initiative. As we get in applications and letters from distraught families, it hurts to think that, unlike my situation where there was no doubt Patrick would get the medical care he needed, their children will not receive treatment until the funds are raised and in place.

I have been so blessed to meet some of these families in person, and I vividly remember one rural father who waited for me to arrive in his province for an entire day so he could express his thanks, which I kept trying to tell him wasn't necessary. We had provided heart surgery for his two-year-old son who was critically ill. He was so in love with this little boy that his feelings took up the entire room. The father was illiterate and couldn't write us a letter, and so he had come in person, riding a crowded bus with the little boy for six hours, to tell me what it meant to their family to know their son would now grow up healthy. He kept telling me how smart his little boy was and how he was determined his son would get an education to have a better life. His gratitude was so transparent and raw that it humbled me deeply. As I left the city that day, he stood quietly on the sidewalk while our van pulled away, gripping his son tightly on his hip and waving his little boy's arm at us until we were completely out of sight.

How I wish that every story of a desperate family had a happy ending. I have had to face the reality that sometimes our very best intentions are not enough. We were once asked to help a little boy named Fu Xiang, whose parents were extremely poor farmers in Shaanxi province surviving on less than 75 cents a day. His mom had cerebral palsy, and, when they gave birth to a little boy with heart disease, they knew they had no possible way of coming up with the funds to heal him. At age five, Fu Xiang was tiny and weak, but he had a smile that simply shone, and oh how he loved his mama and baba. His mother had a heart of gold, and she spent her every waking moment doting on her precious son. His parents had heard that LWB might be able to help their son get the surgery he needed, and so they left their tiny field to travel to the city to apply. When they were told that we would first need to raise the funds for their child's heart operation, they said they would just wait next to the hospital for news, no matter how long it took. Now that they had finally been given renewed hope that their little boy would get his second chance, they said they couldn't leave the hospital grounds until they heard whether or not he was accepted by our program. They camped outside longing for him to receive his operation the moment we made a decision.

School children in the Netherlands heard about Fu Xiang's case and helped to raise the funds required, and the pure joy on his mother's face when she heard he would finally receive medical care was palpable. A few days later, Fu Xiang went into a seven-hour surgery and was then moved to intensive care. As a mom, I sat that night and knew in my heart all of the emotions that his mother was going through while she helplessly watched him through the ICU window hooked to so many machines. Our volunteer team and supporters said so many prayers that his recovery would go well.

And then we got the terrible news that he had passed away in the night.

It's still hard for me to even think about because I keep going back to his mom and dad – and the hope they had that finally their precious son would be healed. It hurt so much to know there was nothing that could be done to bring Fu Xiang back to them. That day I wished I could take his mom's hands and tell her how sorry all of us were that her little boy didn't make it. I wish I had some magic way to bring her comfort, but that simply wasn't possible as she had lost the dearest thing in her life — her only child.

That week, I asked myself repeatedly the age old question of why bad things happen to such kind and good people, and why one life is spared when another is taken. Of course, I don't have the answers. For some reason, we had been able to help countless rural families walk out of the hospital with such joy, but Fu Xiang's family had to leave in complete sorrow, now sadly and tragically childless.

The applications keep coming, and rural farming families keep contacting us with the same desperation of wanting their child to have a chance at life. We have been asked for help by a family who was so poor they lived in a cave, and another who somehow managed to live and eat on just 50 cents a day. The one thing they all have in common though is that they share an agony of wanting to help their child find healing. We can never lose sight of the transformative power of hope, even when we face those moments of sorrow that we can't even begin to understand.

Usually when a family does make the fateful decision to abandon their child, there is no way for us to ever find them again. There have been so many times over the years that we have taken in urgent babies needing surgery, whom we have literally been able to heal within hours of their birth. But then we are left with a one-day-old baby who will now have a healthy life, with absolutely no idea of who left them. I would give anything to be able to find the family and say, "Please come back. She's better now. Please come back and take your child home." But, in reality, those times are few and far between.

One family I will never forget who chose abandonment was baby Corey's, although when he first came into our hands, I never dreamed I would someday know who they were. We were called by an orphanage one night when a newborn with anal atresia was brought in by the police needing emergency surgery. We moved the tiny baby to the hospital right away, and then things got a wee bit more complicated.

Right before his surgery was to take place, we learned that the police had identified who the birth mother was, and that they had plans to arrest her for infant abandonment since she had knowingly left a baby who needed medical care. One of the hospital officials told us that a distant cousin of the woman had been found and that someone would be coming to get the baby, and so surgery was postponed. But no one ever arrived that day, and the little boy remained alone, still in need of urgent medical care.

We then learned that the birth mom was not married and that the father was a migrant worker who had long since disappeared. She had given birth to the little boy and then noticed that something was terribly wrong with him, and so she had panicked and left the tiny newborn outside by the street. When the mom learned that there was a chance she was going to be arrested, she fled to another province where she began hemorrhaging after her recent delivery. While her newborn son was in the local hospital struggling for his life, she was now in critical condition in a hospital two provinces over. Her immediate family refused to help her in any way for having a baby out of wedlock.

One of our team members was able to speak with the relative who had been found, and he said that he simply couldn't help the baby as he was trying to borrow money to pay for the mom's hospital bills. So we found ourselves in the delicate situation of having a baby with known relatives needing surgery, but none of them were willing to care for him or give consent. Sometimes life is just really complex, isn't it? We knew the tiny boy was completely innocent in all of the drama unfolding around him, and so we hired a nanny and told the hospital we would commit to fund any medical expenses he had. We didn't know at that time whether a family member would ever step forward to claim him or whether he would end up in orphanage care if his mom really did go to prison.

Thankfully, the hospital agreed to move forward with surgery, and little Corey sailed through his operation and began to feel better almost immediately. We remained in constant contact with his mom's cousin, sending updates on the little boy and encouraging news of his progress. He finally agreed to come to the hospital and see the baby and promised to pass on the news to Corey's mom that her son was now doing well. We held our breath as we learned that she was finally going to be released from the hospital, and we celebrated when we learned that the police had decided not to press charges after realizing she abandoned her son in panic and not spite. Just a few days later, Corey's mom walked into his hospital room and came face to face with the baby she had last seen when she put him down on the sidewalk. She was at first very nervous to pick him up with his large incision, but soon he was cradled in her arms – right where we knew he belonged.

We got to know Corey's mom very well over the next few weeks while he was in the hospital, and, of course, we understood that her circumstances had not magically changed. She was still an unmarried mom in a country where that is a very difficult road to navigate, and she still lived in poverty, working as a cook at a temporary construction site. But one major thing had definitely changed in the last month, and that was her commitment to raising her son. She told us of the shame she had felt when she realized what she had done, and she wanted to thank all of the kind-hearted people around the world who had not given up on her little boy. She promised that she would never leave him again, and we pledged to cover the next surgeries he would need so that he could grow up strong and healthy. Absolutely, they still had many challenges in front of them, but we saw a real commitment in her eyes on the day she returned. After the doctor told her that Corey would soon have a normal life, she began to weep, telling us that his cries on the day he was born had torn open her heart. Each time we would check on Corey and his mom after he was discharged, we could see that their bond was such a strong one. It is many years later now, and they are still doing well. We give thanks that we were able to play a part in helping them be reunited as that rarely comes to pass.

As I think of the countless babies we have taken into our programs who have been left on their own, I come back to the debated question of whether someone who abandons their child deserves to be honored. My mind goes back to a weekend many years ago when I was making breakfast for my kids. I had made them poached eggs, and, just as I picked up the pan of boiling water to move it to the sink, my son TJ came running around the corner and collided with me. Steaming hot water poured over his head, and I immediately knew that he had been burned. As the blisters on his scalp began to appear, I realized that, for the first time I could remember, I was the one who had caused one of my children to be seriously hurt. Obviously, with as many kids as I have, there have been lots of times they've been injured, but this was the first time I felt a deep sense of responsibility that I had directly caused their pain. Throughout the day, as I held him with tears streaming down his face, I tried to put words to the range of emotions I was feeling inside. I could never properly describe it, but it was a mixture of panic and heartbreak and a deep, visceral ache. I had caused this.

As I sat holding him in my arms that day, for some reason my mind kept going to his birth mom. All afternoon, as my own heart was hurting wondering if TJ was going to be okay, I just kept imagining what it would feel like to carry a child inside you for nine months and then have to set that baby down and walk away. Or what it would feel like to have an extended family member come into your room after the delivery and take your child away from you forever. When I thought I had hurt TJ, it was one of the worst feelings I had experienced. I kept wishing I could turn back time and have that moment over. If only I would have waited five more minutes to clean. If only I would have turned the other direction heading to the sink. If only... if only... if only. But there was no way to change what had happened. It was done, and my son was the one impacted.

Thankfully, in our case TJ was soon back to running around, albeit dosed on Motrin and with a huge gauze bandage on his head. While I still felt such sorrow that I was involved in his injury, I got to hold him and hug him and know he was going to be okay. How very different for his birth parents who have no idea whether he is safe, loved, or even still alive today.

I simply can't imagine the feelings that must come with giving birth to a child and then not knowing what became of him or her. How many times during the course of your life would you lie in bed at night and wish you could turn back the clock as well? How many times would you wish you could get that moment back and perhaps do things differently? If only your extended family would have accepted your child's special need. If only you had the funds to provide your child with the medical care needed. If only... if only... if only. But then the realization would wash over you yet again that there is no way to change what had happened. It was done, and your child was the one impacted and gone from your life forever.

Yes, I'm absolutely sure that the nannies are correct that some who choose to abandon are "bad people" and truly don't care whether the child lives or dies. But I still worry that tens of thousands of birth parents in China each year carry that deep feeling of sorrow in their hearts that I felt when I burned TJ, multiplied exponentially since they have no way of knowing if their child is now okay. How often does TJ's birth mom think of the son she brought into this world, with a shockingly full head of black hair? What I wouldn't give to let her know that he is loved beyond measure. TJ is my son now, however, only because a family in China wasn't able to keep him, and I only get to love him because someone else experienced great loss. It is for those reasons that, as I hold him in my arms, I will forever hold his birth parents deeply in my heart as well. And, for as long as we're able, I'll continue to be grateful whenever we can take some of the anguish away from desperate families who watch their children become increasingly sick due to a simple lack of funding. The relief they feel when they know someone else cares whether their child lives or dies is so immense. I have heard repeatedly from parents we've helped that they will now raise their children to know there is true good in the world, and that they will teach their children how important it is to help others like they were helped. Tiny seeds of compassion and caring can grow into an impact we have no way of measuring. When we're able in any way to help prevent abandonment and keep a family united, those are times when the best prayer I can lift to God is simply, "Thank you."

Twenty-One

This is Community

I think one of the hardest things for me serving as the official head of LWB is that people often want to give me credit for everything that is happening for the kids in our programs. I want to go on record to say that is so woefully inaccurate. The reality is that none of our work takes place without an entire community of people coming together, and that is honestly one of the most incredible parts to me of this life-changing work. We're bombarded every day with media stories of all the bad in the world and how our current society is going to heck in a hand basket, and yet I get to see each and every day the most beautiful and tender acts of mercy from people all over the world.

Right after I adopted my daughter Anna, I had written to several charities working in China to see if I could volunteer in any way because I felt I wanted to do something to help other children in my daughter's homeland. I remember getting several responses back that they didn't really have any volunteer opportunities available, which, of course, wasn't what I was hoping to hear. So when LWB was first getting started, it was very important to me that we create a place where people with a real passion for helping children could get involved. It has been amazing to watch it unfold. While LWB now has a small number of paid staff members, essential to running a charity with the size of our programs, volunteers remain at the very heart and core of our work. They run healing homes and arrange surgeries and help create schools. They write child reports, chart weight gains, and send thank you notes to donors. From pilots to professors, moms to financial advisors, the wealth of experience that these dedicated people bring to our work is extraordinary.

I've always been a firm believer that if you don't know the answer to a problem, then you need to ask for help. I have probably said the words, "I need your advice," more times than I could count as we've created new programs. The wonderful thing is that with very few exceptions, people respond back with, "How can I help?" – and thousands of people have helped LWB since its inception, each leaving their own special mark on our history. You really need to believe me when I say with complete conviction that people are awesome. Magical things take place when people come together to try and make a difference in the world.

LWB has never had a brick and mortar office building because we never wanted to limit who could get involved by location. Our work is done virtually, using a myriad of ways to connect internationally, from video conferencing to phone calls to what I'll admit is often an overwhelming number of emails. When planning care for a child with a special need, it isn't uncommon to have a volunteer in Iowa Skyping with another in Spain, who is coordinating with a volunteer on a small Australian island, while talking to a team member in China. Yes, we give thanks for the Internet each day, while also recognizing how wonderful it is that the children in our programs are truly loved around the world.

I have been told by corporate professionals that there are a hundred different reasons why our set-up shouldn't work, and yet since the beginning it has. I believe that one of the major reasons is because we all remain committed to building an authentic COMMUNITY around the children we serve. We want to "do life together," with the kids foremost in our minds, and that feeling of being part of something so much bigger than ourselves keeps things going strong. We share stories every day with each other about the great kids in our programs, like proud moms and grandpas, celebrating when they head to school for the first time or join a foster family, and comforting each other when a child is far sicker than expected. We've had volunteers from over 20 countries give their time to help coordinate programs for us, and financial gifts to help the children have come from generous people worldwide. I continually get to see the very definition of love without boundaries being given to orphaned and hurting children from around the globe, and I never take that for granted.

One of the little boys who illustrated the amazing power of community was little Yong from Guizhou Province. When he was just four years old, he was found all alone, most likely abandoned due to the enormous facial tumor which had disfigured the entire right side of his face. The staff at the local orphanage where he was sent tried many times to get him the help he needed, taking Yong to hospitals in Guizhou, Yunnan, and even Shanghai, but they were told the mass was just too rare and complex to treat. The next year, his tumor began growing even more rapidly and started to impact his ability to swallow and chew solid foods. Knowing there was a real possibility the massive growth could soon close off Yong's airway, his orphanage contacted us and asked if there was any way he could get medical treatment overseas since the hospitals in China had said surgery couldn't be done there. We didn't know if that would be a possibility, but we said we were willing to try.

Soon after, I posted a photo of Yong on our Facebook page, asking if anyone knew of a hospital that would possibly take his case, and the outpouring of support was overwhelming. In the photo I shared, Yong was wearing a checkered shirt and jean overalls, and he was making a peace sign with his tiny fingers. At that point, the tumor was so enormous that we actually had people accuse us of photoshopping the picture. Literally hundreds of individuals emailed and phoned us to ask how they could help. We had complete strangers calling hospitals in Boston and Miami and New York. I received letters from people in Europe offering to contact the top medical centers in their countries as well. In the meantime, we arranged for an MRI to be done locally in Yong's home province, and surgeons and radiologists in the U.S. and London examined the images we received. When we were told that the tumor might be malignant due to its rapid growth, we sent Yong to another hospital in China to have a surgical biopsy done. We were so thankful when the results came back that the tumor was benign, but we knew that his life was still in jeopardy if it continued to grow at its current pace.

A few weeks later, we received the wonderful news that Yong had been accepted for care at a major children's hospital in Los Angeles. We only needed to raise the funds for his surgery and arrange for a medical visa. The operation would be extremely complex, of course, as his was a type of tumor which had only been seen a few times in recorded medical history. Many of his facial nerves had been stretched in major ways, and doctors worried about how to save his ability to swallow and show facial expressions. The blood supply which was feeding the aggressive tumor would bring special challenges to the operation as well. Because of the magnitude of this first surgery, the bill would be enormous. Of course, hospital care in the United States is far more expensive than in China, but even the deeply discounted charity price for Yong was still going to be $100,000. I'm pretty sure when I heard that number that I stopped breathing for a few moments, but it was clear that the tumor was going to cut off Yong's air supply soon, so we moved forward in faith that the funds could be raised.

In early February 2013, in partnership with the Kim Clement Center, we posted our first plea for little Yong, and the community which rallied around him left me in tears. In just four days, thousands of people stepped forward to raise the funds for his surgery costs. In just short four days. We received notes and letters from around the world, and each one sent the beautiful message that saving Yong's life was vitally important. We heard from kids like Lauren and Jacob from Kentucky who emptied their piggy banks to donate $15.62. Incredible kids like Natalie, who saw Yong's photo and created a website encouraging people to skip eating out for one meal and instead donate to help him receive surgery. Donations came in from around the globe, including Granada, Singapore, Spain, and more. We heard from children who asked for donations to Yong instead of birthday presents, college kids that apologized because they couldn't donate more than $20, and grandparents donating in honor of their kids. An incredible, astounding community of strangers, all united around one five-year-old boy and all celebrating that he soon would receive the help he needed.

A few weeks later, we received news that I certainly wasn't expecting. We received a call saying that due to a new national policy involving orphans leaving the country, Yong would NOT be able to travel to Los Angeles for surgery. No medical visa would be issued. I was devastated by the news, and I struggled to understand why the wonderful plan which had been put into place for Yong couldn't come to fruition. I knew without a doubt that we were running out of time to get him the help he needed as his oxygen levels were dropping, and he had stopped gaining weight. I also wondered how we would tell those who had donated for him the difficult news that the surgery would not be taking place in California. Everyone following his story was waiting with such hope for Yong to board the plane to America. That was an easy one to figure out, though, because we simply told the truth – that we were completely surprised by the decision and that we would, of course, refund every penny of their donation, if they desired.

Our volunteers were incredible during this time, writing to each and every person who gave with a sincere apology, even though there were thousands of people to contact. I was the most worried about all of the children who had opened their hearts to help Yong. I think it's so essential to encourage compassion and giving in even the youngest kids, and it hurt to think that this news could perhaps be difficult for them to understand or even disillusion them. I know many of our donors felt such a myriad of emotions, from sadness to anger, to confusion and concern. But once again our community showed me the goodness of people's hearts. Almost every donor told us to keep the funds given for Yong in order to help the next child waiting in line for medical care. So while Yong wasn't able to come at that moment for surgery, many other orphaned children received life-saving care in his place instead.

I flew immediately to China following the news that Yong couldn't come to the U.S. to meet with officials about how he could still get the help he needed. It was there that I got to see community in action once again, from his wonderful foster parents to local doctors to government staff, who all wanted to work in unison to make sure he could finally receive treatment. Together, we all agreed that Yong's absolute best chance at healing would come through adoption. He needed a permanent family, with access to quality medical care, who could stand beside him for the complex and possibly lifelong treatment he would need. Within weeks, his adoption paperwork was finalized and sent to the national government for approval, and at the exact same time a wonderful family stepped forward to commit fully to Yong's adoption…Kim and Jane Clement, the same couple who had first offered to help him get to LA for medical care. In a beautiful twist of irony, through that adoption Yong ended up permanently in Los Angeles, where he underwent surgery by the exact same medical team and hospital who had offered to accept him originally. It was wonderful to see yet again that God was fully in control the whole time; there were just a few extra twists and turns on Yong's journey to California.

Another wonderful example of real community came through a newborn girl named Pearl. She was found at just four days old with a hospital note stating she had a meningocele, a large "spinal tumor," which is actually a protrusion of the membranes which cover the spinal cord. Although we don't know for sure, like many other babies abandoned with medical needs, there was a good chance that Pearl's birth parents were unable to afford the medical treatment she needed. Babies born with this condition usually need urgent surgery as the outcome for any baby with a meningocele is better if surgery takes place before the bulging sac can rupture. We made arrangements with her orphanage to move Pearl to Shanghai immediately, where the skilled neurosurgeons at Fudan University could repair the opening in her back.

Our plans to help Pearl get surgery hit a snag, however, when the hospital ran initial intake tests and discovered that

Pearl's blood type was Rh negative. In China, negative blood is very rare; less than 1% of the Asian population has this specific type. At the one children's hospital where Pearl currently waited, over TWO MILLION children are seen there each year, and so the blood supply needed in just Shanghai alone is immense. As one volunteer told me, people in China with negative blood have a "valuable and rare substance flowing through their veins." Unfortunately for Pearl, the city's blood bank was completely out of Rh negative blood at that moment, and so the doctors were unable to perform her emergency surgery.

In all of our years working with children needing medical care in China, we had never run into this problem before. The more we researched, the more we learned of the great need by hospitals for this specific type of blood. And then something truly remarkable happened. When our supporters heard that Pearl was unable to have surgery, friends from all over the globe began contacting people they knew in China to see if anyone had negative blood they could possibly donate to help Pearl. Word spread quickly on the Internet that an orphaned baby was in need. In less than 24 hours, over 30 people volunteered to donate their blood to help her. Isn't that incredible?

While there are Chinese regulations in place which prevent people from donating directly to an individual (since there are often long waiting lists of patients needing this type of blood), enough donors came through in Shanghai that day that all the patients ahead of Pearl received the blood they needed, and then it was her turn as well. She had her neurosurgery the following day and sailed through the operation perfectly – another beautiful example of how community can change someone's life in very real and significant ways.

I know a lot of people are still hesitant to take that first step to get connected with a charity's work, however. I remember getting a letter once from a woman who was considering whether or not to support LWB. She asked a question I have actually asked myself in the past: "Why are so many children hurting in our world?" She went on to write that the enormous need made her feel quite overwhelmed, and she actually wondered whether anything she could do would really make a difference in the grand scheme of things. With millions of orphaned children around the world, it's easy to think our own individual efforts won't matter. It's also easy to get caught up in that age-old question of "Why?" Why are children born only to be abandoned? Why doesn't every child have access to medical care? Why do so many children have to grow up feeling alone, without anyone truly invested in their lives?

After doing this work for so long, however, I have realized that there are no clear answers to the question of "why?" But I have also realized that the much more important question to ask at that point is, "What now?" Our attitude towards that question tells an awful lot about ourselves and how we view the world.

There will always be naysayers who feel our individual efforts are fruitless when the issues of child welfare and poverty are so immense, but I know without a doubt that, to the one tiny baby lying in an orphanage crib sick and alone, our response is essential – and our answer needs to be "YES."

Yes, we will try. Yes, your life is important to us. Yes, we will do everything possible to let you know the meaning of the word "hope." When you join those individual efforts into a team and then a community, the good that happens in the world is profound.

I have also had people tell me in the past that they're afraid to get involved in helping orphaned children because they think it will hurt too much to become invested in their lives. I can understand this, of course, because I know firsthand how much it hurts when a child you're trying to help becomes sick or even passes away, but I still can't imagine not trying to help them. I told a friend once that this work is like standing on the shore of a frigid, icy lake, with a distant island of love and warmth in the middle. If you just put in one toe or finger, you would feel the deep cold of the water and be afraid to ever get in. Easing in slowly doesn't always work well either as you would get about up to your waist and think, "I don't think I can do this." When it comes to trying to save the life of a child, there is only one way to go – and that's by plunging in. Take one deep breath of faith and dive in completely to try and help them. That's the type of community I get to experience every day; people diving in to help as many children as possible. We'll never be able to answer the question of why so many children around the world live in such need, but we can BE the answer to individual kids who are hurting when we join together to bring them hope.

I am especially encouraged when charities work together in community to make sure as many kids as possible are served. I read a quote once that said something like, "It's when we start working together that the real healing takes place." We've been blessed to work alongside so many other wonderful groups in China, and it's definitely true that the children are always the winners. While LWB can help with many different medical needs in China, for example, we don't have anyone trained on the ground who can do club foot casting, the treatment of choice for babies born with feet rotated in at the ankles. Any time we get a child into our care with this special need, in order for them to be helped we need to ask another charity for assistance. One of the wonderful organizations also doing orphan work in China is a group called Little Flower, based outside of Beijing, and they are experts at casting. Baby Pearl, who had rallied people to donate their Rh negative blood so she could have surgery for her meningocele, had also been born with bilateral club feet. Soon after she recovered from her surgery in Shanghai, she made the journey up to Beijing to stay at Little Flower, where in just a few months they got her precious little feet realigned. Pearl then graduated from their home into our foster care program in Anhui, where she will remain until she is hopefully chosen for adoption. I love thinking about how many people have invested in her life so far, particularly since so often orphaned children have almost no one in their corner. She has no idea yet at the tender age of one just how many people have been cheering her on, but I hope someday I can share with her the story of how everyone came together to make sure she was loved.

I can't end this chapter without giving a very special thank you to the community of people on the ground in China who make sure that the kids in our programs get the very best care possible. I think there is often a tendency with charities working in foreign countries to mistakenly come across as, "We're here to save the day." That goes against everything we believe in at LWB, and we never want to convey a message that somehow we know how to do things better. Our goal from the very beginning was to connect with as many local people as possible who share the same dream of helping children have a better life. We have always wanted everything to be a partnership, working side by side on projects that could make a real difference to children and orphanages. I am so grateful that we have such a strong system in place now that when I suggest something totally Western and unrealistic as a possible idea, our Chinese team members can laugh at my plan and tell me to think again.

Without a doubt, it's our incredible team of local citizens throughout China who are the ones on the ground changing lives every day, and their commitment to the kids is second to none. Our hospital manager in Shanghai, for example, is a retired man who travels 90 minutes each way to visit the kids having surgery and speak with the doctors about their progress. When nannies travel from far away regions, he meets them at the train station, day or night, ensuring they get checked into the hospital ward okay and making sure they have all the supplies they'll need. When there have been times that a nanny has become too tired to keep working, he steps in to watch the baby himself. There have been many times that he has personally taken a child being discharged from the hospital in Shanghai to our healing home in a different province, traveling many hours by train with the infant to make sure the baby is delivered safely. He also gives very good advice to the nannies arriving at the hospital when needed, such as the time one older woman brought a large cardboard box with her to the ward and placed it next to the baby's bed. When the box began moving side to side and making clucking noises, our manager patiently explained why bringing a live chicken to the hospital probably wasn't a very practical idea.

I wish there was a way for anyone who thinks of China as just that one collective word to meet our staff and volunteers throughout the vast country. They have devoted their lives to making a difference in the world, and their friendship is something I will treasure forever. One of our foster care managers is a young mom named Mei. She is a school teacher during the week, but every weekend she travels by bus, taxi, or a borrowed motor scooter to visit children in our foster homes. She told me that it often takes her from early morning until late at night to see all the kids as the foster families live so very far apart. She goes regardless of the weather, carrying boxes of rice cereal and formula to deliver to the kids, often standing on the side of the road in the falling rain or snow waiting for the next bus to arrive to head to the next foster home. She recently had a new baby, and, when I asked her if she needed to step away from the manager position, she replied that the job was so important to her. She told me, "I want my new daughter to grow up seeing that helping others less fortunate is an essential part of giving thanks for one's life." We've been blessed with similar team members all throughout China, and together we bridge any cultural differences to bring real hope to the kids.

Community is such a blessing, and it is something that I believe God wants all of us to have. I read once that the greatest social issue facing Americans is loneliness, and I think we all can probably pull up a time in our lives when we felt completely alone. It is one of the worst feelings in the world, and it is one of the reasons why we try our best to make sure orphaned children have an opportunity to be chosen for adoption – so they can become a treasured part of a family. No one should go through life alone.

I have tried to raise my own kids to know that the key to having a rich and fulfilling life is to follow Jesus' two simple commandments: Love God. Love people. It's really that easy, but we as humans continue to make it oh so hard. We want to exclude and build barriers and make excuses on why we shouldn't reach out to others, but those four little words can truly move mountains. Love God. Love people. When we can do that, especially when we unite for the common purpose of helping others, then the community that develops and grows is not only genuine, but life-changing.

Twenty-Two

Jasmine

When LWB first began, it was to save the life of one little boy born with heart disease – a collective effort to heal an orphan's heart. What I have discovered along the way, however, is that it was my own heart which was ultimately changed forever by the thousands of children I have been honored to meet along the way. I wish I could tell you about every one of them because each child who has come into our hands is such an incredible gift to the world – although reading a 10,000 page book would probably be a lot to ask. I have to share just one more child's story with you, though, because Jasmine, the young lady it involves, is such an enormous inspiration to me.

In March of 2011, I walked into an orphanage in western China and heard the children who lived there singing a welcome to us from one floor above. As I came up the steps and into the main room, my eyes were immediately drawn to a young girl in a wheelchair whose smile lit up her entire face. She had two little ponytails sticking out on each side of her head, and there was just something about her which brought an immediate aura of goodness to my mind. When I knelt down to meet her, I was told that Jasmine had been brought to the orphanage when she was eight years old, after losing the use of her legs. Once again, it was painful to think about the emotional hurt abandoned children go through when they suddenly find themselves on their own in an orphanage, but I tried to push those thoughts aside so I could concentrate fully on the beautiful little girl in front of me, who had the sweetest smile. Within minutes, it became clear that she did indeed have a very loving personality as I watched her make sure that the younger children crowding around us all got their share of the snacks and treats that we had brought. She wanted to make sure that no one was left out. By the end of our time in her rural town, she had embedded herself in my heart, and I said goodbye to her, worrying about what her future would hold. Jasmine was already 12, and she had never received an education since she was confined to a wheelchair. Neither her orphanage nor the town where she lived was handicapped accessible at all. I knew that her future would most likely involve being institutionalized forever, and that was something I just couldn't accept for this beautiful young girl who so clearly had an exceptional spirit.

Jasmine's orphanage thankfully prepared her adoption file, but, because of the many unknowns about her muscle and limb weakness, no family at that point had stepped forward. We started a small school program in her orphanage, and we watched as Jasmine turned 13. Then the worry over her future intensified in our hearts because we knew on her very next birthday she would become forever ineligible for adoption. I know many LWB team members had a lot of sleepless nights wondering what more we could do to spread the word that this remarkable young lady was waiting for a permanent home. We wrote blogs and shared her photo on Facebook, and we prayed and then prayed some more. One day in 2012, a wonderful family saw her picture, and God whispered to their hearts to look deeper and more closely.

Dan and Lisa were already adoptive parents. When I heard their story, I knew they were the perfect family for Jasmine. Dan was a physician in the Midwest, and many years previously he had been called to consult regarding a baby whose birth mother had decided to give her up for adoption while the infant was still in utero. An adoptive family had been selected, but when a subsequent ultrasound showed that the baby girl would be born with a severe heart defect, they immediately backed out. Soon after, the birth mom signed papers saying that she didn't want any medication which would keep her daughter alive continued, and so it seemed that the little girl would be born and pass away soon after.

Dan was so troubled by this story, and, soon after the baby was born, he went to see the little girl himself. He told his wife Lisa that he had taken one look at the baby's tiny toes and fallen in love. As he examined the newborn, his heart was burdened that that there was no sign of celebration or joy over her birth in the sterile hospital nursery. Dan went down to the lobby gift shop and bought several stuffed animals to place in her bassinet, and he wrote orders in her chart that she should be picked up and held every hour by the nurses. Soon after, Dan and Lisa made the decision to bring baby Hope home to their family for as long as she had to live, and adoption became a part of their lives. They went on to adopt additional babies and toddlers who had medical needs as well, this time from China. They had never really considered an older child adoption, however, before seeing Jasmine's picture. In fact, they had made the pointed decision that adopting an older child wouldn't be right for their family, for dozens of different reasons.

The truth is that older child adoption is most definitely not for everyone, and it absolutely is something that should never be entered into lightly. I have seen firsthand many well-meaning families who raced in to "save a child from aging out" whose lives dissolved into chaos after the adoption. Those who consider older child adoption, or any adoption for that matter, need to do so with their eyes wide open. We can never forget the reality that every adoption only occurs through a child experiencing both trauma and loss. And every year that a child spends fending for himself in institutional care, or being shuttled through foster families, only adds to the complexities of integrating into a now permanent home.

One of the confounding things about older child adoption, however, is that just as every human is unique, so is every adoption experience. There simply isn't any way to know which children will embrace becoming part of a permanent family and which will use their survival instincts to fight tooth and nail against ever trusting another adult again. I have seen older children who came from the hardest backgrounds of neglect blend almost seamlessly into their new families, and I have seen children who I thought would do beautifully in a permanent home rage, fight, kick, terrorize, and self-harm as their hearts in childhood had been wounded too deeply. I still remain a huge advocate of older child adoption because I believe so strongly that everyone deserves a family, but no one should make that decision lightly, and every family has to prepare themselves for walking into a great unknown.

Dan and Lisa educated themselves in every way they could for the adoption of a teen, and they began gathering all the paperwork required as quickly as they could since the clock was inching closer to Jasmine's 14th birthday. With literally just two weeks to spare, they finally found themselves in Jasmine's province signing the adoption paperwork to make her their daughter forever. I was so happy to get an email from them saying she was even more amazing, remarkable, and wonderful than the day I had first met her in the orphanage. Lisa wrote, "No one leaves her presence without being moved." My heart was filled with so much joy that Jasmine's future was now going to be unlimited. Little did I know then how Jasmine's kind and unselfish heart was going to continue expanding my own.

All during the adoption trip, Dan and Lisa kept asking Jasmine if she had any questions. Again and again, Jasmine would shake her head and say no. She had no questions at all, until the final day, when she turned to their Chinese interpreter and spoke quietly. The guide suddenly began to cry as she translated Jasmine's words. Jasmine's only question was this, "Can anyone take me away from my family when we get to America?" That fear of being abandoned yet again was still deeply in her heart.

As Jasmine began learning English once she was home in the U.S., more of her life story began emerging for her parents, and a lot of her experiences caused them to weep. They encouraged her to write down and share her thoughts as one more step towards healing her past. With their and Jasmine's permission, I am sharing some of her journals. I want you to remember as you read her words that there are thousands and thousands of Jasmines living in orphanages around the world today, and their stories deserve to be heard.

I wasn't an orphan when I was born. My grandma and grandpa took care of me, not my mom and dad. My parents visited me once or twice (at my grandparents). My grandma was very nice to me. However, my grandpa liked to drink, and then he would hit me. However, one day my life changed.

One time when I was in school, my grandma came to get me before the class ended. I thought it was strange. She and the teacher talked a little bit, but I didn't know what they were talking about.

When we left, I asked her why we left so early and she said we were going to see my brother. Then I was very happy! My grandma and me rode a couple of hours. Then there was a man who took us to an office. I didn't know why they took us to the office. It was still a mystery to me.

When they finished talking, I was very happy because we were going to see my brother. However, when we got there, what I saw wasn't my brother; it was a lot of kids. That's when I realized that it was an orphanage.

I cried when I asked my grandma to not to leave me there, but she didn't look at me at once. Why did she lie to me that we were going to see my brother? I can't imagine that she lied to me. At that time I was eight years old and I was very scared.

I don't understand why she abandoned me. I asked her many times when she left me, but she just left me and then she was gone.

Jasmine had spent three years in the orphanage before I had met her, essentially confined to a wheelchair and unable to even leave the floor she was on as the orphanage only had stairs and no elevator. No one in China knew what her medical condition was. Testing in America has now given the sad news that she has a very rare form of muscular dystrophy. There are no surgeries that will "fix" her medical issues; her muscles will continue to decline. But the nannies in her orphanage didn't understand this, and the doctors she saw there told the orphanage staff there wasn't any reason why Jasmine shouldn't be able to walk. She was told repeatedly she was simply lazy, and her life in the orphanage was a difficult one.

One time in China the nannies say I can walk, so they test me, put the food over where I can't reach it. The nanny says if you can reach it you can eat, and if you cannot reach it you cannot eat and be hungry. I try all day and I can't reach the food. I really hungry. The nanny hit me and say, "You can't reach it and I have to do everything. You should walk. Why you cannot walk?" I just cry and can't say anything.

In China, at the orphanage I can't drink because people say I will have to potty lots and they don't want to take me to the potty because I too heavy. Sometimes I sit on potty chair all day because they don't want to take me to the potty. Sometimes I sleep on the potty chair at night because they don't want to lift me on the bed because I too heavy. Sometimes I think I could be not heavy and then everyone can carry me and they won't be mad at me. I want to go potty by myself but I can't.

Sometimes the nannies won't take me to bed because they don't want to carry me. They just let me sleep on the floor. They don't give me blanket or anything. At night I very cold. I not sleeping really good because it is cold and the floor is really hard. They tell me I should come up to bed. I can't stand up but they say I can walk. Sometimes I feel like nobody care about me. If one day I could walk everything would be so good. I could walk and do everything and the nannies wouldn't have to help me. I wouldn't get yelled at and the nannies would like me, but I can't do anything.

There were many people who told me I am lazy. Actually I really want to walk because I want to help people! When a new nanny came, she would ask me, "Why you can't walk?" I didn't know how to answer. I don't know why I can't walk. Then a nanny answer the new nanny, "Because she is lazy, she said if she walks, then we can make her do things." When I heard the conversation, I was very sad. I didn't say that. But they just won't believe me.

Why they don't believe me? Why? What I say is all true, but they just don't believe me. They hate me a lot, they also don't like me. Why they saying things like that to me? I don't understand why they don't like me. Is it just because I am a person with a disability? The nannies told me I'm so lazy, but I want to stand like other people too.

The life in the orphanage made me so scared and so sad. I once made a wish saying, "There's only one thing I want. I just want a family, I really really only want to have a family. Just to have people who care about me, people who love me, people who like me."

Sometimes I was really happy when I saw other kids being adopted, I was truly happy for them. Sometimes, I would be very very sad thinking that I would likely never be adopted. I would feel very very bad. But sometimes I would think, it's a very good thing that there are kindhearted people who adopt orphans!

I was really scared that I would not have a chance anymore once I was 14 years old. I was afraid that when someone wanted to adopt me it would already be too late. I didn't know someone would adopt me, this I really didn't know?

I didn't know if there would be anyone who wanted me.

I also hoped lots of kids would be adopted and would not have to keep suffering here. Some kids were so afraid, many kids wanted to be adopted. Sometimes I would say, "This is not my home, I want to have a family of my own."

How grateful I am that Jasmine's wish for a family came true. Once Dan and Lisa made the decision to adopt Jasmine, they sent a care package to her orphanage, like so many adoptive parents. Dan included a letter to his daughter-to-be, and before he wrote it, he prayed a lot about what it should say, knowing these would be the very first words she would ever hear from him. He started the letter by saying, "To my beautiful daughter." Months after Jasmine was home, she shared just how much that letter meant to her as she had been told repeatedly how worthless she was. She said she had taken the letter out again and again to read her new daddy's words, crying as she read them and taking them into her heart to store. The nannies would see her reading the letter and say, "What if they don't make it in time, before you turn 14?" Jasmine would reply, "They are coming. My daddy told me so." And, of course, Dan and Lisa did come, and they give thanks to God daily for blessing them with such an incredible daughter, even while their hearts break for all the years they missed with her. Jasmine's writing continues:

"In China people say I cannot get adopted because I cannot walk. But one day they told me that a family did want to adopt me. Mommy and daddy thought I had spina bifida, but the paperwork was wrong. I have something else. When mommy and daddy see me on adoption day they thought I had muscular dystrophy. After mommy and daddy meet me I was really worried that they would take me back to the orphanage. The nannies told that when my mommy and daddy saw me they would take me back because I cannot walk. In China you have 24 hours to decide if you want to keep the kids or not.

But mommy and daddy didn't take me back to leave me there. They took me back to the orphanage to hand out clothes that mommy and daddy had brought for the kids. The kids were so happy when I handed out the clothes. It was so much fun!

I come to America and I have back surgery for my scoliosis. After they did a muscle biopsy, the doctors know I have spinal muscular atrophy (SMA).

When I was in China, I thought no one could love me because I couldn't walk or do anything. But after that I tell mama and she said, "She doesn't love me because I can do anything." Mama said that she fell in love with me the first time she saw my face. Daddy said the same thing.

Before they saw my face, mommy and daddy had said they would not adopt older kids. They said they wouldn't adopt anyone over 4 because it wouldn't work in the family. But mommy and daddy saw my face and fell in love and thought God was saying "that is your daughter".

This year has been hard for me because I think mommy and daddy will leave me too. I think it would be better if everyone else hate me so my heart won't hurt again. I try to make everyone mad. Mommy and daddy said they know I do this because I am afraid they are going to leave me so I want to leave first.

But now I know mommy and daddy won't leave me because I said bad things and made everyone mad but they still love me and forgive me.

I believe I have a purpose and God has a plan for me. I don't know what all I will do yet, but I know He has a plan.

Aren't her last lines so profoundly beautiful? Jasmine has been through more in her young life than anyone should have been through. She has faced abandonment, physical punishment, scorn, and ridicule. She watched as her body stopped doing the things she wanted it to do. She lost the ability to walk, the ability to lift herself – but Jasmine never lost her inner goodness or compassion for others. In fact, her experiences made her even more determined to help those who are living through the same things she did. Because she felt great hunger, she never wants another orphan to go without food. Because she experienced cold, she wants orphans to have blankets and warmth. Before she had her spinal surgery in America, as the doctor was putting her to sleep, he asked her what it was she wanted when she woke up. Without a moment's hesitation, Jasmine said she wanted there to be no more orphans.

In 2015, she and her sisters Grace and Elyse launched a project entitled "Jasmine's Dream," with the audacious goal to help 1,000 orphaned and impoverished children find hope and healing. Jasmine and her sisters want to help orphans that are in danger of aging out and to help fund surgeries through our Unity Initiative so that families can stay intact. They are well on their way of reaching that first goal. This amazing trio has made the commitment to donate their weekly allowances, and they are selling bracelets, cookies, and artwork – all to help the kids who are left behind. They are living a life of purpose, and Jasmine's heart inspires not only me, but people from around the world. I can't wait to see what else they will accomplish and how many lives they will go on to touch.

Twenty-Three

Living Out Our Name

Now that LWB has such a trusted presence in the charity world, we receive letters almost daily from orphanages and groups around the globe asking for help. We hear from desperate families in rural Asia and small orphanages in Africa and local NGOs in Central America, all asking for assistance for the children in their care. For years I would read these letters and feel a weight in my heart, wishing that there was some way we could make an impact in their lives. From around 2009 on, each time the Board of Directors for LWB met, they would discuss whether it was time to move our programs beyond China, but at every meeting the decision was made to wait just a bit longer.

I would occasionally send through some of the more poignant requests to our Board, and I kept a file of small local NGOs who had contacted me who appeared to be doing transformative work, with the most meager of resources. Then in April of 2016, I woke up to the international headlines that the government of China had passed a new Foreign NGO law, the "Management of Foreign Non-Government Organizations Activities in China." In a nutshell, all foreign charities must now register with the Public Security Bureau, China's national police authority, for approval to conduct their activities. In addition, the new law states that all charities must now work under the supervision of a "mother-in-law" organization, an official Chinese agency who will oversee any activities done in the country. A widespread feeling of panic began spreading throughout the foreign charity world as everyone waited for news on what the new national law would mean for those running programs in China. I read everything I could possibly find on the new law, and our team members in China began speaking with everyone they could about what would be required in order to keep our life-changing programs open, but as of the time I am writing this, we still don't have additional news.

The reality about all of life is that it can change in the blink of an eye, can't it? People go into their work in the morning, business as usual, only to learn in the afternoon that their job has been eliminated. An accidental fire can consume a house in no time at all, leaving a family who had no worries the night before suddenly homeless. A woman can walk into her doctor's office after a routine mammogram and learn everything about her health has completely shifted in the time it takes to hear the devastating news. All of life is about change, whether we want it to be or not, and I had to start contemplating the reality that the new law might make it impossible for us to continue helping children in China in the same way we had in the past.

Needless to say, I did a lot of praying in the spring of 2016. I had been helping children in China for the last 13 years, and some of our volunteers joked that I had jinxed us all with the new law because in early March I had actually made the decision to cancel our annual directors' meeting because everything was going so smoothly in our programs. Our surgery program was working with the top hospitals in China. Our foster care programs were continuing to impact lives in major ways. Our school programs had added dental and nutrition components, and more children each year were transitioning from the orphanage schools to regular Chinese public school. I literally called our head of operations and said, "There's no reason to bring everyone together for a meeting this year because everything is going perfectly." I guess I forgot to knock on wood.

As I reflected on what the future now held for LWB, I kept returning to those three little words I had heard way back in 2003: **Every child counts**. God had placed those three simple words deeply in my heart, and countless times over the years as we made decisions on which programs to launch I would hear them play over and again in my mind. Every child deserves a chance. Every child deserves to know love. Every child deserves to grow up hearing that their life matters.

I also began realizing that just as I was completely comfortable with my life as a stay-at-home mom all those years ago, I was also now completely comfortable with helping children in China. The fear and uncertainty I had experienced as we launched each of our new programs in the early years had been replaced with knowledge and confidence that real help could indeed be given. I lived and breathed the Chinese charity world now, and as quickly as a child would come into our intake process, I would usually know right away what the solution was on how to help her. While the needs of the children were still often enormous, the programs we had put into place were running pretty seamlessly.

In May of 2016, the LWB Board met to discuss the possible impact of the new law and to once again ask the question of whether it was time to take the very successful children's programs we had created to other countries. This time it was unanimous that we needed to live up to our name and move beyond the boundaries of China. Our commitment to the children of that country remains solid, as we believe there is still so much to be done to help those being abandoned with medical needs. It is our sincere hope that we will be allowed to continue our programs and work side by side with our local partners there, as lives are still being saved every day. I know, however, that there is a global child crisis as well…with millions of innocent children living in poverty, hunger, and with a feeling of hopelessness.

While my own journey of helping children began with the adoption of my Chinese daughter, I know all around the world there are amazing children asking the same types of difficult and heartbreaking questions she did: "Why did my parents leave me?" "Why can't I go to school?" "Does anyone even care that I'm here?" So once again I had to ask myself if I was ready to step completely out of my comfort zone. Were we ready to go back to square one in order to help children in locations I really only knew on a map?

I began talking with local people all over the world who are trying their best to impact the vulnerable children in their communities. I researched countless websites and read everything I could find on which countries had the most at-risk children. I prayed for wisdom and guidance, and I felt God's comforting message that, "Yes, it's now time."

That is how I found myself standing in a rural village in Uganda on a hot August day, getting ready to go with the beautiful children there on their long and often dangerous daily trek to collect water. We had chosen Uganda because we knew the needs there were immense, with over 1.2 million children orphaned by HIV alone. The country's health indicators are among the lowest in Africa, and sadly many preventable diseases still take a major toll.

I had already been told that the children in this particular village had to walk a very long way to fetch water each day. I knew that for the younger children and women who were elderly or heavily pregnant, it could take up to four hours of their day. EVERY single day. But I also knew it was one thing to hear it, and another to live it, and I think the village elders were taking bets on whether or not the foreigner would make it down and back up the mountain. I tried not to take it personally when they ran to get me a "baby water can" to carry, because they were so confident I would never make it back up with a normal sized one.

From the moment we started down the steep dirt path, we began to meet children slowly walking back up who had already been down to the water source. Many of the children begin their first morning water trek in the dark, being guided only by the light of the moon. I was told that a 20-liter water can weighs 40 pounds when full, and yet almost every child I passed had one on his or her head. I was also told that from the moment a child learns to walk, they learn to carry water. For as my new friends told me repeatedly, "Without water...there can be no life." How very much we take for granted here in America. I will never look at my kitchen faucet in the same way again.

It was on this trip to Uganda that I was shown once more that every child on earth has a story that deserves to be known. So many of the children that I met were malnourished, without even a pair of shoes to their name, and yet they welcomed me to their village with exuberant singing that still echoes in my mind today. I met nine-year-old Michael, whose parents had died of HIV and who after their deaths found himself living alone at the town landfill. His life had been filled with so much sadness and loss, and yet he still dreamed of becoming a doctor when he grew up so he could help people "get better," since his parents had not. He watched me closely when I pulled out a box of crayons, and finally graced me with a shy smile when I invited him to help me color a picture of a rainbow fish. We sat on the dirt quietly coloring in shades of blue and purple and green, and as I watched his earnest concentration to stay inside the lines, I understood clearly that as an orphan, his innocent childhood hopes would be crushed far too quickly without some type of encouragement and support.

I met eight-year-old Mary, whose mother had been violently killed, leaving her and her siblings living in a tiny mud hut in abject poverty. I learned that Mary lived with almost constant hunger, but she came right up to me on that first day and smiled, showing off her dimples and cementing the tragic knowledge in my heart that far too many children in this world are living without a feeling of safety. What could they accomplish if we came together to show them how important we believe their lives are?

A few weeks after my trip to Africa, I flew to Cambodia, where we walked barefoot through the mud, in intense rainy season downpours, to visit children in several rural villages there. If you're like me, much of what you know about Cambodia probably involves the Killing Fields and the Khmer Rouge, a devastating period in their history which resulted in the deaths of almost two million people, or an unthinkable one-fourth of their population. Cambodia became, in the far too simplest terms, a country of trauma, with the effects of the Civil War still impacting their society today. Life in the impoverished rural villages there remains difficult, with many having no electricity or running water, and a staggering 40% of children under the age of five being malnourished.

On this trip, I visited the notorious border region between Thailand and Cambodia, where children every day face the horrific issues involving child trafficking. I thought I had prepared myself for what I might see and hear, but as I listened to the stories of children who'd been broken, my heart filled with a deep sadness. Many of the villagers now refuse to let their children walk to the government schools, as they are up to 10 km away. It's just too dangerous for the small children to make the daily journey due to the presence of traffickers. And yet without education, the children in this region have absolutely no chance of ever escaping poverty.

As I sat and listened to them explain this dilemma, I couldn't help but flash back to the day all those years ago when Dr. Huang in the Shantou orphanage asked that fateful question, "If the children can't go to school...can we bring school to them? I already know the answer to that one thankfully, and we're very excited to get started. Every child certainly does count, and I can't wait to see where else we can live out that truth.

And so I come to the ending of this part of LWB's story and once more to a new beginning. I look back on the journey so far and thank God for opening the doors He has for us. I'm a completely different person now than I was back then. I like to think I'm a wiser person because I understand now how very little I actually know about this complex and often messy place we call the world.

I have also seen along the way that humankind is truly extraordinary. We might each be unique in our DNA or our customs or opinions, and yet there is a collectiveness of emotions which each of us share. Throughout our lives, all of us will experience joy and excitement but also sorrow and regret, regardless of the country of our birth.

I remember standing on the shore of the ocean one evening as the sun went down, watching the beautiful golds and reds as it dipped closer to the horizon, and I turned to look at the others who had made their way down to the water to experience the close of day. On almost every face I could see wonder and reflection. I turned to the person next to me and said, "I was just thinking about how many people over the ages have stood on this shore at sundown, contemplating life," and the woman next to me said, "I was thinking the exact same thing."

After being blessed to meet people around the world through my work, I believe there is a common center in each of our souls. We all want to feel loved and accepted and that our lives matter. I think we're born with hearts of grace, willing to trust others, but then life has a way of causing our emotions to become tarnished and our feelings to harden. People let us down; life isn't always kind and, in fact, is sometimes cruel. I have seen that firsthand through my work, far too many times. Yet someone will then come along who shows us again so clearly the exquisiteness of what humanity can be.

My work with orphaned and abandoned children has taught me, that from our very first breath on this earth, we need each other. How would things change if we could all remember that simple fact? I like to think we would be kinder and more patient with each other. That we would set a goal to be more fully present with those around us.

It is an extraordinary gift to meet people who remind us that the world can indeed be a wondrous place. They challenge us to be the best possible versions of ourselves, don't they? So let's be like Jasmine and her sisters and set bold and glorious goals to help those around us, even if people say it's not possible. Let's be like Dr. John Padilla and encourage others just starting out to "Dream big, dream big, dream big." Let's reach out and lift up and try to shine a little brighter in this fast-moving world which often leans to darkness.

I close this book now in the memory of all of the children who have left this life far too soon. I will carry you in my heart forever and remind myself that each day we are given is a precious gift. No matter how much we like to think we're invincible and that we have unlimited time, the reality is that each of us gets but one single life. The real tragedy comes when we waste it.

For the millions of children who are living right this moment inside orphanage walls – children who would give anything to feel valued and wanted – let's not take the blessings we've been given for granted. Let's give thanks for all the people who care about us today and look outside ourselves a bit more to see those around us in need.

Through the heart of an orphan, my own heart has been transformed. I hope their stories have touched yours as well. The incredible children I've met on this journey remind us all that when we come together with unconditional love…absolute miracles occur.

For more information on Love Without Boundaries and our work with vulnerable children, please visit

www.lovewithoutboundaries.com

"Every Child Counts"